THE

JUST

WORSHIP

SERIES

It's Glory

Becoming the Victor Rather than a Victim

Steven Excel Deaver

Excel Publishing Company
A Division of Excel Media and Music Group
New Jersey

THE

JUST

WORSHIP

SERIES

It's Glory

Becoming the Victor Rather than a Victim

© Copyright 2007 by Steven Excel Deaver

Published by Excel Publishing Company
A Division of Excel Media and Music Group

P.O. Box 902
Piscataway, NJ 08855-0902
ISBN: 0-9720025-0-2

Cover Photograph: Ris'shan Shamar Leak

First Printing 500 copies July 2009/Worldwide Distribution

TABLE OF CONTENTS

FOREWORD

I want to commend Steven Excel Deavers' book The Just Worship Series: It's Glory to the world and the body of Christ. He is indeed a growing prophetic voice for the 21st Century. It is my joy to release him to the body of Christ. The Just Worship Series is designed to share with its readers the principles and keys of worship and spiritual warfare through prayer, prophetic worship and the proclamation of the word. As a covering elder for Cathedral International adjutant's ministry, he has walked out a victorious and overcoming lifestyle before us all, as well as ministered to my needs as a faithful son.

Steven's life has been seasoned by personal trials and triumphs, but the deep roots of his Pentecostal rearing from his sainted mother has proven to keep him steady through the storms of life. You will see this as you read his book.

You will find in this reading a four stage biblical plan of action for surviving and overcoming during end times, discover what joy and glory really are and how God has designed these kingdom principles to propel your life into total victory.

I am sure his perspective on how the church should respond to the present day historic and future world events will be a blessing to you. While all may not agree with his perspective, they are worth reading and certainly you will find yourself encouraged thereby.

Bishop Donald Hilliard, Jr.
Senior Pastor – Cathedral International

INTRODUCTION

I am greatly honored to write the introduction of this book. First, because I am the wife of the author and I love and respect him dearly. Secondly, his passion for God has compelled me to seek a new dimension in worship.

When I first met Steven, it was evident that there had been some struggles in his life. However, one look into his eyes revealed what was going on in his soul. It was as if God was saying "Do not be moved by the struggle, there is more than what you see." Man looks on the outer appearance but God looks on the heart. During some of our most challenging moments – when the enemy desired to sift us as wheat, Steven would gravitate to worship and after he had been strengthened – he would strengthen me.

It was obvious to me that I had a jewel who loved the Lord with all of his heart, soul, mind and strength through his lyrics such as: "Teach me how to worship, Oh how I love Your presence and I want to be like You" just to name a few. II Chronicles 16:9a says: "For the eyes of the Lord go to and fro upon the earth looking for someone whose heart is perfect toward Him" and I safely respond "Have you considered my husband?"

Through worship, Steven has become a spiritual giant who does not fear the onslaught of the enemy. He definitely is a part of God's end-time generation, the Davidic generation which has been assigned to usher the Body of Christ into the restoration of all things kingdom.

So relax and take this exciting journey. You will thoroughly enjoy, be encouraged and supernaturally empowered by the revelation knowledge in this book.

Theresa I. Deaver

DEDICATION

To my mother, the late Prophetess Maggie Bell Deaver, for all the times you brought the family around your bed to pray and worship, and for teaching me to love the truth; then showing us how to live the truth; and finally, for toiling with me until I learned how to walk in that truth.

ACKNOWLEDGMENTS

Thanks to my best male friend, Preston Hughes, for being there for me and to my covenant brother and faithful friend, James Washington, for under girding me. Just Worship through your storms, there is peace on the other side.

Thanks to Moses Banks, Tim Shider, Eric Parker, Helene Harrison, Stacie Long, Cookie Drayton-Price, Steven Walker and James Washington for sharing your vocal and music gifts on the first Just Worship CD.

Special thanks to Regina Timmons for always being available to accommodate all of my ideas on paper, and without whom, my manuscript would not have been ready for publishing. You are my quiet encourager.

I am grateful for family and friends who helped sustain me through my wilderness journey, in particularly, Hosea and Chauncey Brinson, Patricia and Roy Chestnut, the late Dr. Josephine Walston, James Chester, Jean Herring, Al Leak, Hervey and Ann Lewis, Egbert Burke, Ursula Whitehurst, Phil and Lisa Kearny, K&S Tire Service, for their financial and emotional support of this project.

Thanks to Lachelle Wong for all your assistance, Carol Dortch-Wright, Patrice Troutman, Rebecca Simmons and Evie Norton for your gift of editing, proofreading and gentleness.

Thanks to Bishop Marvin D. Williams for your example and showing me the purpose of a family covenant.

Thanks to Bishop Samuel M. Leak for the opportunity to serve on a national level in the body of Christ.

Special Thanks to my spiritual parents Bishop Donald Hilliard, Jr. and First Lady Hilliard, for being a bridge to my divine destiny and understanding that my past pains were my purchases for my present glory. Theresa and I will always honor and love you. Thank you to the Cathedral International Pastoral Staff, and the entire Church Family, especially Pop and Mom Rodgers.

Certainly not last, to my wife and best friend, Theresa. Thanks for your love, support and patience. After worship, it's you alone who can pull my heart string.

Finally, I thank my children Ris'shan, Ibn, Alexis, Jamal, Ameerah and Steven Excel II, and my grandchildren, Destiny, Faith and Isaiah Jeremiah. You're all blessed, highly favored and deeply loved of the Lord. Remember, great is your peace and you all will be taught of the Lord.

THE WORD OF THE LORD

Growing up in an American culture, whether it's in the rural farmlands of Kansas, the suburban coastlines of California, or the inner cities of Los Angeles and Detroit, we Americans have come to accept the fact that to dial the numbers 911 means there is an emergency situation at hand. Therefore, I think it not strange that some have labeled and called the greatest-American tragedy, the World Trade Center and Pentagon bombings, 911 too. We all know that the numbers nine and eleven when combined represent the date of this historic event. However, it is something of far greater significance - this event was not just a signal of a natural emergency, but it spoke volumes of a spiritual 911 call for this nation. And, let us not take lightly the recent Virginia Tech Massacre. Our nation, especially our youth, is in a spiritual and moral emergency. We are at the crossroads of maintaining our allegiance to God Almighty as a Christian nation or choosing rather to redefine our nations' history by forging political and international alliances of compromise under the disguise of world peace. Hear the word of the Lord America; **we must not wither but we must worship Christ as Lord**.

This book not only assists you in finding a right perspective on looking at and looking forward after September 11, 2001, you will find some revelation for that focus in this book. However, as you read through the pages of this book you will also find some prophetic direction and much more some spiritual comfort. This book, will challenge you in sojourning far beyond this natural tragedy but it will also give you guided hope and faith to overcome our nations' spiritual tragedy – a failure to truly worship Jesus Christ.

I believe that the 911 and same sex marriage events are just the start of a wave of additional world wide crisis events – political, religious, social and economical – to be "utilized" by God to reveal His glory in the earth through His church. I stress utilize because God does not cause evil, neither is there any evil in Him. **God is a good God**. I truly believe that God is merely responding to our sinful nature as humans with His goodness and grace. Yet, make no mistake about it; this is the body of Christ's finest hour. In spite of great darkness in the earth, she must

"Arise, shine; for her light has come, and the glory of the Lord is risen upon her. See, darkness covers and

thick darkness is over the peoples, but the Lord rises upon you. Nations will come to your light, and kings to the brightness of your dawn" (Isaiah 60:1-3).

Come and go with me on a personal, prophetic journey as I share with you how to Just Worship and come to experience the place of glory, where God's plan to be a victor rather than a victim is revealed. While many people are in despair, you can cast all your cares on the Lord, Just Worship Him and not just see the glory but you can be the glory.

PRELUDE

Souls are being lost daily. Sadly enough, it doesn't have to be that way. Salvation to many is a myth. People find it perplexing to believe that they are saved by the word of God when their lifestyle is inconsistent with their confessions of love and devotion to a gracious Savior. Why?

They mistake position in Christ with possession of Christ-likeness, which is a developing process. The world looks at the church from afar and mocks and scoffs at her because they feel that things are better for them than they are for the faithful. However, the new millennium will reveal to all the satanic deceptions that the late 1980's and 1990's have perpetuated on those who did not receive the engrafted word of God – the power of salvation, and those who outright rejected Christ.

Child of God, it is true today, yesterday and forever: righteousness, peace, and joy in the Holy Spirit are three pillars and hallmarks of the kingdom of God. Although the world is entangled with unrighteousness, confusion and depression, as we embark on the new millennium, the true church of the living God now have a revelation and a restored soul that possesses the goodness, grace and the glory of the Lord, and because He decreed it, we can declare and decree what He decreed, and He and all of heaven will demonstrate what we declare in the earth, according to His word.

INTERLUDE

Oftentimes God spoke to the prophets of old and asked the question, "What do you see?" To God it was a rhetorical question because He possessed the answer for it beforehand; it was He who gave the prophet insight into the Spirit realm.

God still speaks to contemporary prophets in order that they may speak to the people. Therefore, the true purpose and power of this book is found in my mere obedience to the voice of God, "Tell my people to Just Worship as I reveal my glory in the earth." The prophetic insights, the word of the Lord and prophetic worship lyrics in print and in recorded songs, are all different messages from God, which I have stewarded for many years in the wilderness. Now He (God) has released me to release them into the earth.

I am not a songwriter, and I am not naturally gifted to write books, rather I am just a steward of the anointing of God, which has many expressions and manifestations. To that end, Lord, glorify Yourself with the same glory you revealed to me in my wilderness experiences.

A CALL TO WORSHIP

God expressively and clearly speaks to and through His creation daily. He calls us to acknowledge (to act-on-our-knowledge) that He alone is worthy to be praised and worshipped, from the rising of the sun to the going down of the same.

Throughout history, the Sovereign has called sinners, saints and society to worship. At different times and eras, the theme song has changed with the culture. There have been musical eras, such as Baroque, Classical, Renaissance, Romantic and Contemporary. I believe that the last musical era will be a synthesis of all of the prior styles, joined with a new style which is so unique to the human ear that only Spirit-filled saints will be selected as stewards of this part of God's heart. (I know secular music will still exist but it will only represent the counterfeiter, satan).

This musical style will be so precious that satanic attacks will come unbeknownst to the vessels and channels of delivery, in an attempt to prevent it from ever being released into the earth. Nevertheless, just as Satan and his kingdom of darkness could not stop Jesus Christ from coming into the earth, he also cannot stop this new style of worship from being released into the earth. It is beginning to happen even now. Yes, there is going to be intense spiritual warfare for the heart and souls of men. But, I believe God is raising up, by His Spirit, a group of Warriors in Worship: a selected group of warring, praising, and worshipping saints who will usher in a release of a newer glory, a greater goodness, and an abounding grace of God, as never witnessed before on earth.

Prophetically, God calls them to worship with a battle cry:

> **Arise all ye warriors**
> **Arise all ye warriors**
> **All ye warriors arise**
> **All ye warriors arise**
> **With the sword of the Lord**
> **We will sound our battle cry**
> **As we enter the heavenly doors**
> **Let the chains of bondage**
> **Fall to the floor**
> **Just let the chains of bondage fall.**
> **[See this complete prophetic song in Chapter 12]**

Chapter One

JUST WORSHIP

"Although the fig tree shall not blossom, neither shall fruit be in the vines; the labour of the olive shall fail, and the fields shall yield no meat; the flock shall be cut off from the fold, and there shall be no herd in the stalls: Yet I will rejoice in the Lord, I will joy in the God of my salvation. The Lord God is my strength, and He will make my feet like hinds feet, and He will make me to walk upon mine high places" (Hab. 3:17-19).

Many people, Christians as well, are perplexed about the uncertainty of our economy, the completing days of 2007 and beyond, the nations of the world discussing war and the imminent worldwide terrorist dangers. God has already unmistakably provided answers, peace, and stability for all who would prescribe to His plan and way of doing things.

God's antidote for these present and last day crises can be summed up in one word – **presence**. He wants us to be able to tap into, and love to experience the glory, the power, and the peace of His presence. There is a place – a secret place that we can journey to through worship and self-surrender where all answers by revelation and glorious manifestations return with triumphant joy. How do we arrive at this place? **Just worship!**

Let me share with you how this works:

"Therefore being justified by faith, we have peace with God through our Lord Jesus Christ: By whom also we have access by faith into this grace wherein we stand, and rejoice in hope of the glory of God" (Rom. 5:1-2).

I am strongly convinced that God's remedy for a saddened and suffering soul is found in the act of worship and discovering His glory. However, in order to begin this act and discovery, we must come to an understanding of three concepts: **(1) justification, (2) journey, and (3) joy.**

In **justification**, we learn that provision has been made for us to have access by faith to approach the throne of God. This access-pass reconciles us with God and causes us to be in a peaceful relationship with Him. All of this is transacted by faith in the atoning work of Jesus Christ; and by His now resurrected and intercessory work at the right hand of God the Father. Having agreed with these terms, we have access to saving grace and we rejoice in Christ in us, which is the hope of glory. The believers' hope is to see God's goodness and grace in every situation. Through the good and the bad, during the happy and the sad, God still reserves the sovereign right to manifest His goodness and grace on the just and the unjust. He has mercy on whom He will. This is a manifestation of glory.

Then, there is the **journey,** which may be described as our everyday experiences in our new found kingdom-the kingdom of God, the kingdom of light. This is in direct counter distinctiveness to the kingdom of satan-the kingdom of darkness. Each opposes the other in a quest to receive the loyalty, attention, and worship of man. Worship is all about relationship. God desires to bring us joy, peace, and righteousness while satan seeks to cause us grief, confusion, and unrighteousness in an attempt to get back at God. The best way to upset a father is to mess with his children. So, on the journey of life, we are tempted by satan and his kingdom of darkness with the lust of the eye, the lust of the flesh, and the pride of life. He seeks for us to come into covenant with the things of darkness and to place our trust in this temporal world. He seeks to steal, kill and destroy our relationship with God. Thus, as we relate and trust more in the creation rather than the creator, we will become idol worshippers. Only true worshippers can relate to God as a father. Idolaters are lost and their identity is found in the thing not in Christ the king. God, rather than us, initiated a blood covenant with us by His son Jesus Christ's shed blood for our personal identification on the journey of life just as He did with the children of Israel throughout their journey into the Promised Land. On their sojourn into the Promised Land, they offered blood sacrifices at each place to reinforce their trust in their covenant with God, Jehovah, and God manifested His character in different ways by revealing to them new covenant names. David, the great worshipper, recognized this principle when he wrote in Psalm 20:7,

> *"Some trust in chariots, and some in horses: but we will remember the name of the Lord our God."*

Justification has more to do with our covenant and faith than with our actions. The moment we truly understand this concept, we will better comprehend that the journey is a prescribed or specially ordered path for us to get to know Jesus Christ in a personal and intimate way. This is why Jesus died on the cross. We did not shed any blood on the cross of Calvary; we just bear our cross here on earth. This is why we also must bear our cross daily (Luke 9:23).

What is the purpose of the cross for you and me? The cross helps us to personally identify with Jesus Christ. It allows us to get to know the anointing.

Receive this revelation of the cross, child of God:

C – Christ
R – Revealed through our
O – Obedience
S – Suffering and
S – Sacrifice

Remember, without the cross, which we are asked to take up daily, there would be no real relationship with Jesus Christ. It would all be a religious, surreal fantasy. But I am glad that I can say, "I know that this thing (salvation through Jesus Christ) is real." The old saints would say, 'He's real in my soul.' So don't despise your cross, rather glory in it. It is the cross you bear that makes you who you are in God and in the body of Christ. Not who knows you or who praises you; no, it is the cross that God knows He has assigned you to bear for His glory.

Therefore, we will not be as successful as we should be against the kingdom of darkness without our last concept tool, which is **joy.** When we synthesize our justification beliefs with our journey of life's principles, (the crosswalk) we must end up with this mindset, I am being filled with Jesus' joy. I am going through tests and trials because by Jesus' shed blood I am **J**ustified or **J**ust like my elder brother (Christ is the firstborn of the saints.) Therefore, I must walk in the footsteps of Christ, he was full of joy. Consider Isaiah 12:3,

> *"Therefore with joy shall ye draw water out of the wells of salvation."*

3

With joy, we receive a reservoir of deliverance and wholeness from the Spirit of God. Consider Nehemiah 8:10,

> *"Then he said unto them, go your way, eat the fat, and drink the sweet, and send portions unto them for whom nothing is prepared; for this day is holy unto our Lord: neither be ye sorry; for the joy of the Lord is your strength."*

It is the Lord's joy that gives us strength to remain on our crosswalk. Where does this joy come from? It comes from the indwelling of the Holy Spirit and the word of God.

> *"These things have I spoken unto you, that my joy might remain in you, and that your joy might be full"* *(John 15:11).*

Do you see it? We live out our Christian life by faith in the work of Christ and in the words of Christ. This brings continual, realized justification.

> *"Behold, his soul which is lifted up is not upright in him: but the just shall live by his faith"* *(Hab. 2:4).*

It is our belief in God's word that brings about our justification as we, with joy, travel on our pilgrim journey; we receive strength for victorious living. And as we journey on in this Christian walk, we must bear our cross which reveals the reality of our salvation. However, if we fail to realize that we must glory in our cross, we will be lacking in the proper supply of the Spirit of Christ to draw on the things that pertain to salvation. Worship and faith are the primary ingredients needed in order to live a victorious, Christian life. How we worship tells how we truly believe and relate to His word and His name. Moreover, it is the joy of worship or the joy of the Lord (the act of Jesus dying on the cross was the ultimate act of worship, obedience, suffering, and sacrifice ever known) that gives us strength to serve the Lord, and not satan.

What was the joy of the Lord? The writer of Hebrews says it was the cross that Christ endured (Hebrews 12:2). As believers in Christ, this should also be our resolve, to despise the shame and guilt of our crosswalk by being full of joy. **Joy will give us the victory because it is a by-product of real faith**. Jesus states that, He spoke His word, His promises, and His covenant to the disciples that their joy might be full (John 15:11).

When we are full of joy we are full of the Word. When we are full of joy we are full of God's Spirit. When we are full of joy we are full of victory. So what is joy? I like to look at it this way:

J – Jesus
O – Orchestrating
Y – You

- It takes Jesus to direct and strengthen your heart to worship and rejoice when things are going backward.
- It takes Jesus to motivate you to praise and worship when you've been recently divorced; your loved one just died; all your money is gone, bills are past due, and there are no groceries.
- It takes Jesus to guide you when seemingly all hell desires to kill you, the people in your house and church, and all the people on your job are working along with hell's plan.

This is why the Prophet Habakkuk, a minor prophet who was historically connected to some aspects of temple worship, could prophetically declare in his prayer in the opening verse of this chapter what God had already decreed. This word is for us today as it admonishes us to wait on the Spirit of God to demonstrate whatsoever we declare, in accordance with His word. He declared victory in this prayer. He declared joy in the text and he declared strength to overcome. He stated if the fig tree shall not blossom, I will just worship. If the fruit do not be in the vines, I am still going to just worship. If the job of getting olives and making and selling oil and the fields shall yield no meat, I will just worship. Can you and I say that with the same boldness and confidence? Or do you worship only when things are all according to your satisfaction. Habakkuk challenges us to become a true worshipper. He tells us to let the Lord be our joy and strength in life and then, and only then, can we stand steadfast and unmovable and, we will indeed walk upon our high places of victory to the praise of His glory. **Having problems – Just Worship!**

Take your time in examining these true worshipper prerequisites before you, like myself, proceed to own the title of being a worshipper. I must admit that it was my personal prayer for God to "teach me how to worship" that brought in such measures of correction and conviction before He started to reveal His wisdom to me.

The first request I had for God was to receive a clearer view of the definition for worship. What is worship? In order to answer that question sufficiently, the Spirit of God gave me illumination in the form of an acronym of the word **worship** itself:

W – Willing
O – Obedience and
R – Reverence to a
S – Sovereign
H – Holy and
I – Immutable
P – Presence and Power

Worship is when we willingly show obedience and reverently honor the sovereign, holy, and unchangeable presence and power of Almighty God. God realizes that we are inadequately equipped to truly honor Him the way He deserves to be honored, so He exchanges our weakness for His strength. He tells us what to say to Him. He already knows it's true of Himself, so the glory and power of His presence that we experience is for us to bear witness that we are indeed communicating in spirit and in truth. We are exactly talking to God and He is talking back to us and Himself through us and by the power of His Holy Spirit.

The next insight revealed to me was **worship keys** to access heaven. Based on the principles found in John Chapter four, (the story of Jesus' encounter with the Samaritan woman), as you go into the next Chapter you will find that I have utilized three subheadings to break up the entire text:

I: **The Reasons We Need Worship**
II: **The Route to Worship**
III: **The Results of Worship**

Get ready, you are about to learn how to get "in joy."

JUST WORSHIP KEY

The believers' constant prayer should be: Teach me how to worship and truly honor Thee, and not what I think worship should be. "Teach me how, what, when, why and where to worship."

Chapter Two

WORSHIP KEYS TO ACCESS HEAVEN

"Ye worship ye know not what...." (John 4:22)

Being that I grew up in, and was nurtured in, an old fashioned tongue-talking, foot-stomping, demon-chasing, spirited-singing, Pentecostal, praying, and preaching church, I thought I had a very real idea of what worship in heaven must sound like. It was not until I left Brooklyn, New York for Orangeburg, South Carolina and arrived at the campus of South Carolina State College (currently a university), that I began to learn of different styles of worship. It was only recently (to my own shame – I would say five to six years ago) that I truly understood that worship consisted of more than just praise and worship or singing songs. Although I was in a church that used a "Call to Worship" style format for Sunday services, in my mind's eye, I really did not comprehend that the entire service, not just Praise and Worship – or what we used to call Devotional Service – was a part of worship, too. I was totally transformed and conformed in my mind about what worship consists of. God has been renewing my mind in this area on a consistent basis, and every time I think I have arrived, I am led to read books by the likes of LaMar Boschman's, <u>Future Worship</u> and Robert Webber's, <u>Worship A Journey into His Presence</u>. These are just a few books that God has used to upset my traditional worship concept and to bring me into a paradigm shift in worship.

The following two chapters are devoted to some strong revelatory and practical scriptures which assisted me in my search to know who, what, where, how and why I worship God through the person of Jesus Christ. Just as Jesus told the Samaritan woman, "ye worship ye know not what," He showed me that I really only served Him from a religious relationship rather than a revealed relationship.

Here is how the Holy Spirit challenged me to really measure whether or not I was a true worshipper. He asked me these five (5) questions:

1) Do you speak the truth in your inward parts?

David, the great worshipper and measuring rod of modern day worship, provides the answer to two rhetorical questions regarding worship in Psalm 15.

> *"Lord who shall abide in thy tabernacle? Who shall dwell in thy holy hill?"*

The answer returned to him,

> *"He that walketh uprightly, and worketh righteousness, and speaketh the truth in his heart."*

I always tell people no matter how much you fall into the sin of not telling the truth, you always want to tell yourself the truth because when you lose this ability, you are really lost.

2) Can you swear to your own hurt?

In that same Chapter, David says,

> *"He that sweareth to his own hurt, and changeth not."*

I found out the reason God did not help me when I was in trouble or in a mess a lot of times is because I did not think I was in trouble or in a mess. Therefore, I did not confess my fault and I did not ask God for help. Even after we are convicted, sometimes we would rather deny that wonderful us could possibly be in error. It's foolish pride. But child of God, if you and I want God's best, we must confess it (whatever it is) to the hurt of your own pride and open up the channels of true worship.

3) Are you a tither?

When I started coming into the deeper things of worship, I began to enjoy the glory and presence of God like I had never experienced in that way before. I longed to be in His presence daily. But then one time, like other times, I missed returning my tithes to the Lord and I gave just an offering. So God began bringing me into conviction and correction. He took me to Proverbs 3:9,

> *"Honor the Lord with thy substance, and with the firstfruits of all thine increase."*

I already knew and sought to faithfully practice Malachi 3:10, but God took this opportunity of my unfaithfulness and disconnection to teach me that not paying tithes was not just being disobedient, I was also failing in the area of being a true worshipper. Tithing is really more about a clean and surrendered heart, than it is about our small change (whatever we give, it's little to God.) Do you believe that you are a great worshipper? I think you need to examine if you are also a tither because along with raising your hands, you must return the tithe to God as an act of worship. Not tithing can hinder true worship.

4) Do you offer sacrifices of joy?

The Psalmist says in Chapter 27 verse 6,

> *"...therefore will I offer in his tabernacle sacrifices of joy..."*

Do you conveniently worship God when things are well and everything is going in your favor, or do you worship in spite of your circumstances and during your tests and trials?

5) Do you have the power of the Holy Spirit dwelling within you?

Jesus brings forth a principle in John 4:22-24 that I think a lot of people miss. He unequivocally states that they who really worship God would understand that God is a Spirit and in order to worship Him we must do it in spirit and in truth. Every spirit is not filled with truth; in fact, only the Holy Spirit is called the Spirit of truth. Only when the Holy Spirit indwells our spirit do we have the ability to discern, to know, and to operate in truth.

Let's go to the scriptures to further explore the art of true worship. You can find the complete set of **Worship Keys to Help Uncover the**

Mysteries of Accessing Heaven in this text: [John 4:4-54]. However, let me make a few statements to guide your thinking.

- The believers' constant prayer should be "Lord, teach me how to worship." Teach me how, what, when, why, and where to worship.
- True worship is not something that we do but rather as we are willing to pay obeisance and reverence to a sovereign, holy and immutable (unchangeable) presence and power, God (Himself) takes abode in our spirit and worships Himself.

Now, let us plunge into those three subheadings I mentioned in the previous chapter and lift out some key principles and insights:

I.   THE REASONS WE NEED WORSHIP
John Chapter Four, verses 4 – 14

"And he must needs go through Samaria. Then cometh he to a city of Samaria, which is called Sychar, near to the parcel of ground that Jacob gave to his son Joseph. Now Jacob's well was there. Jesus therefore, being wearied with his journey, sat thus on the well: and it was about the sixth hour. There cometh a woman of Samaria to draw water. Jesus saith unto her, Give me to drink (For his disciples were gone away unto the city to buy meat.) Then saith the woman of Samaria unto him, How is it that thou, being a Jew, askest drink of me, which I am a woman of Samaria? For the Jews have no dealings with the Samaritans. Jesus answered and said unto her, If thou knewest the gift of God, and who it is that saith to thee, Give me to drink; thou wouldest have asked of him, and he would have given thee living water. The woman saith unto him, Sir, thou hast nothing to draw with, and the well is deep: from whence then hast thou that living water? Art thou greater than our father Jacob, which gave us the well, and drank thereof himself, and his children, and his cattle? Jesus answered and said unto her,

*Whosoever drinketh of this water shall thirst again:
But whosoever drinketh of the water that I shall give
him shall never thirst; but the water that I shall give
him shall be in him a well of water springing up into
everlasting life."*

**Note: Feel free to refer back to the above text in a numbered bible
while you are reading, so you can better follow me.**

Key #1 (Verse 4)

Jesus saw the need to go and teach about worship. We will
never grow in worship until we see the need to learn more and
do more when it concerns worship.

Key #2 (Verses 5-6)

There was a preordained place of worship; that place is called
"everywhere." However, God determines "the hour to
worship" in a place. He knows when He deserves glory for
past, present, or future blessings, and how much He deserves.
He knows we are creatures subject to time restraints.

Key #3 (Verse 7)

The woman came to draw water (worship) but she did not
know how to do this just yet nor did she know where to
worship. Her reasoning, her rhetoric, and her race prohibited
her from this knowledge.

Key #4 (Verses 8-9)

She needed an example of how to reconcile relationships. The
disciples went to deal with the carnal need of getting food.
Jesus needed no religious rules to hinder the act of renewing
and the act of re-establishing a divine relationship.

Key #5 (Verse 10)

Jesus showed her that salvation is a gift. Worship is a gift that we receive and once received freely, we freely give it back to God. Many people do not realize that it is a gift; we believe we earned it based on our good behavior or based on our spirituality. God gives us discernment to know when to worship. He gives, therefore, it's a gift.

Key #6 (Verse 11)

She did not understand the power of the human spirit that has the ability to contact God. She lacked knowledge that Jesus was the great connector or the mighty reconciler.

Key #7 (Verse 12)

She only knew religion and could not receive revelation. She did not know the done aspects of relationship, rather only the do part of religion.

Key #8 (Verses 13-14)

She was dead because of trespass and sin and had an unquenchable thirst for it. We need to know that worship taps us into the fountain of life. In summation, we need worship because we are constantly stuck in religion rather than pursuing the deeper waters of a true relationship with Jesus Christ.

Those were some of the Reasons Keys; now let's look at some Route Keys.

II.   THE ROUTE TO WORSHIP KEYS
John Chapter Four, verses 15 – 26

"The woman saith unto him, Sir, give me this   water, that I thirst not, neither come hither to draw. Jesus saith   unto her, Go, call thy husband, and   come hither. The woman answered and said, I have no husband. Jesus said unto her, Thou hast well said, I have no husband: For thou hast had five husbands; and he whom thou now hast is not thy husband: in that saidst thou truly. The woman saith unto him, Sir, I perceive that thou art a prophet. Our fathers worshipped in this mountain; and ye say, that in Jerusalem is the place where men ought to worship. Jesus saith unto her, Woman, believe me, the hour cometh, when ye shall neither in this mountain, nor yet at Jerusalem, worship the Father. Ye worship ye know not what: we know what we worship; for salvation is of the Jews. But the hour cometh, and now is, when the true worshippers shall worship the Father in spirit and in truth: for the Father seeketh such to worship him. God is a spirit: and they that worship him must worship him in spirit and in truth. The woman saith unto him, I know that Messias cometh, which is called Christ: when he is come, he will tell us all things. Jesus saith unto her, I that speak unto thee am He."

Key #9 (Verse 15)

She asked to be taught how to worship. If we think we know, then we are lost, but if we seek and ask, we shall find new rivers or new streams of life.

14

Key #10 (Verses 16-19)

True worship began with transparency and truth within the inward parts.

Key #11 (Verses 19-20)

She confessed her inner confusion and misunderstanding of how to worship. We must do the same.

Key #12 (Verse 21)

Jesus shared that belief is a primary part of the formula and requirement of worship. It is not the place that matters as much as a person's faith.

Key #13 (Verse 22)

All other gods are false gods and idols. Therefore, foundation is essential. Worship begins with Jesus and worship ends with Jesus.

Key #14 (Verse 23)

The way of true worship is now revealed and it's not only to be seen in types and shadows, but in spirit (from the heart) and in truth (God's way). True worship is to be manifested among men.

Key #15 (Verse 24)

We must worship from and with this understanding (spirit and truth). God's gift of the Holy Spirit brings us into the dimension of spirit and truth.

Key #16 (Verses 25-26)

We must believe and come in contact (face to face) with the presence of God (messiah/anointing). When the anointing is permitted to charge and change the atmosphere, we can know all things (we need to know) by a word of knowledge, prophecy, a word of wisdom and discerning of spirits or by the other gifts of the Spirit.

Now that we understand "Route", let's finally examine the "Results."

III.   THE RESULTS OF WORSHIP
John Chapter Four verses 27 – 54

"And upon this came his disciples, and marvelled that he talked with the woman: yet no man said, What seekest thou? The woman then left her waterpot, and went her way into the city, and saith to the men, Come, see a man, which told me all things that ever I did: is not this the Christ? Then they went out of the city, and came unto him. Meanwhile his disciples prayed him, saying, Master, eat. But he said unto them, I have meat to eat that ye know not of. Therefore said the disciples one to another, Hath any man brought him ought to eat? Jesus saith unto them, My meat is to do the will of him that sent me, and to finish his work Say not ye, There are yet four months, and then cometh harvest? Behold, I say unto you, Lift up your eyes, and look on the fields; for they are white already to harvest. And he that reapeth receiveth wages, and gathereth fruit unto life eternal: that both he that soweth and he that reapeth may rejoice together. And herein is that saying true, One soweth, and another reapeth. I sent you to reap that where on ye bestowed no labour: other men laboured, and ye are entered into their labours. And many of the Samaritans of that city believed on him for

16

the saying of the woman, which testified, He told me all that ever I did. So when the Samaritans were come unto him, they besought him that he would tarry with them: and he abode there two days. And many more believed because of his own word; And said unto the woman, Now we believe, not because of thy saying: for we have heard him ourselves, and know that this is indeed the Christ, the Saviour of the world. Now after two days he departed thence, and went into Galilee. For Jesus Himself testified, that a prophet hath no honour in his own country. Then when he was come into Galilee, the Galileans received him, having seen all the things that he did at Jerusalem at the feast: for they also went unto the feast. So Jesus came again into Cana of Galilee, where he made the water wine, And there was a certain nobleman, whose son was sick at Capernaum. When he heard that Jesus was come out of Judea into Galilee, he went unto him, and besought him that he would come down, and heal his son: for he was at the point of death. Then said Jesus unto him, Except ye see signs and wonders, ye will not believe. The nobleman saith unto him, Sir, come down ere my child die. Jesus saith unto him, Go thy way; thy son liveth. And the man believed the word that Jesus had spoken unto him, and he went his way. And as he was now going down, his servants met him, and told him, saying, Thy son liveth. Then inquired he of them the hour when he began to amend. And they said unto him, Yesterday at the seventh hour the fever left. So the father knew that it was at the same hour, in the which Jesus said unto him, Thy son liveth: and himself believed, and his whole house. This is again the second miracle that Jesus did, when he was come out of Judea into Galilee."

Key #17 (Verses 27-28)

When we find true worship we must turn and forsake the old for the new (leave the waterpots or self's way) and do it God's way.

Key #18 (Verses 29-30)

When we become a true worshipper, we possess a greater and more powerful witness for the Lord. We then have the power to receive revelation knowledge and the ability to share it with others.

Key #19 (Verses 31-33)

Worship feeds the spirit and soul as well as it has an effect on the body. Jesus tried to reteach the disciples. They also did not understand all the mysteries and secrets of true worship. We do not either.

Key #20 (Verse 34)

Worship helps us to know the will of God, and encourages and motivates us to do the will of God.

Key #21 (Verses 35-36)

Worship helps us to recognize, reach out, reap and rejoice over the harvest.

Key #22 (Verses 37-38)

Worship changes the atmosphere, which creates an easier harvesting field. Modern day worshippers are living on the seeds of worship sown by the previous generation. We worship for our children and our children's children.

Key #23 (Verse 39)

Worship helps you and others to believe easier. It amplifies our testimony.

Key #24 (Verses 40-41)

True worship will always produce more worship and increase a person's level of faith.

Key #25 (Verse 42)

Personal worship is the primary key to a better understanding and for getting to know the Lord personally. I can't worship for you and you can't worship for me. Every man, woman, boy and girl must worship God for themselves, if they will ever know and be known of God.

Key #26 (Verses 43-45)

The act and effects of worship are universal in principles. It works throughout the world.

Key #27 (Verses 46-47)

Worship heals the sick and delivers us from the point of death. (Note that this was Jesus' second visit to Cana. I deal with His first visit in Chapter 3).

Key #28 (Verses 46-47)

When we learn about worship keys, we will be able to come and go into real, holy, and acceptable worship, at will. We can worship the Lord freely (this expresses our love for God and the Lord's loving response towards us).

Key #29 (Verse 48)

When we become true worshippers, we can speak to the Word (Jesus) and then of the Word (His Promises) in faith without seeing it, and go believing that He will bring His Word to pass.

Key #30 (Verse 49)

We must show our worship by our requests and our actions. The nobleman asked Jesus because he believed that He could do it. We should not look to man to do what only God alone can do.

Key #31 (Verse 50)

After requesting we must go and act on our beliefs.

Key #32 (Verses 51-53)

When we act on our beliefs, then we will know and receive the witness in our ear and spirit. When we do this we will receive the desired results we seek.

Key #33 (Verses 48-54)

Worship not only helps us to believe, but it also helps us to receive the word of God and its benefits.

In this Chapter Jesus gives us dynamic worship keys on how, what, when, where, and why to access heaven. These keys can be utilized if we want entrance into that secret place – His presence.

As I close this Chapter, observe some more "Results" of worship in one of the foremost, scripturally-based results chapters on worship in the bible. It speaks of protection, power and preservation.

Psalm 91

"He that dwelleth in the secret place of the Most High shall abide under the shadow of the Almighty. I will say of the Lord, He is my refuge and my fortress: my God; in him will I trust. Surely he shall deliver thee from the snare of the fowler, and from the noisome pestilence. He shall cover thee with his feathers, and under his wings shalt thou trust: his truth shall be thy shield and buckler. Thou shalt not be afraid for the terror by night; nor for the arrow that flieth by day; Nor for the pestilence that walketh in darkness; nor for the destruction that wasteth at noonday. A thousand shall fall at thy side, and ten thousand at thy right hand; but it shall not come nigh thee. Only with thine eyes shalt thou behold and see the reward of the wicked. Because thou hast made the Lord, which is my refuge, even the most High, thy habitation; There shall no evil befall thee, neither shall any plague come nigh thy dwelling. For he shall give his angels charge over thee, to keep thee in all thy ways. They shall bear thee up in their hands, lest thou dash thy foot against a stone. Thou shalt tread upon the lion and adder: the young lion and the dragon shalt thou trample under feet. Because he hath set his love upon me, therefore will I deliver him: I will set him on high, because he hath known my name. He shall call upon me, and I will answer him: I will be with him in trouble, I will deliver him, and honour him. With long life will I satisfy him, and shew him my salvation."

If you want these results, first seek to explore the "Reasons" and "Routes" of worship; then you will always find access into heavenly places and experience this protection, power and preservation.

JUST WORSHIP KEY

True worship is not something that we do but rather we are willing to pay obeisance and reverence to; a sovereign, holy and immutable (unchangeable) presence and power, God (Himself), who takes abode in our spirit and worships Himself.

Chapter Three

WORSHIP: The Marriage Between Heaven and Earth

"And the third day there was a marriage in Cana of Galilee; and the mother of Jesus was there: and both Jesus was called, and his disciples, to the marriage. And when they wanted wine, the mother of Jesus saith unto him, they have no wine. Jesus saith unto her, woman, what have I to do with thee? Mine hour is not yet come. His mother saith unto the servants, whatsoever he saith unto you, do it" *(John 2:1-5).*

Although I want to focus on the first five verses of this text, I will continue to glean from the spiritual gems found in the entire chapter. In fact, I have divided this chapter into three subheadings much like that in Chapter 2:

I.   **Readiness for Worship**
II.   **Receiving the Spirit of Worship**
III.   **The Radical Results of Worship**

Come along with me as we continue our journey in receiving prophetic insights from this critical subject, which is so vital to victorious Christian living. Before I begin, I want you to please take note that worship is taking place at a wedding feast that is almost an identical event to what will happen with Christ and His church in heaven as recorded in the book of Revelation. Although I am not a musician and I would rather be considered as a steward of the song of the Lord than a songwriter, I am aware of the uniqueness of what occurs when music and lyrics come together to make a beautiful song. It's like a man meeting a woman and after a few dates and conversations, he knows that she is the right woman for him and that he wants to marry her. This is exactly what true worship in the presence of the Lord is like. Again, I am not a musician, but I can hear music and I can discern if the musician has married a song with the notes or heart of God. I do not know how all of this transpires, but I do know when it has or has not happened.

Let us look at how to prepare for worship.

I. Readiness for Worship
John Chapter Two, verses 1-6

> *"And the third day there was a marriage in Cana of Galilee; and the mother of Jesus was there: And both Jesus was called, and his disciples, to the marriage. And when they wanted wine, the mother of Jesus saith unto him, They have no wine. Jesus saith unto her, Woman, what have I to do with thee? mine hour is not yet come. His mother saith unto the servants, Whatsoever he saith unto you, do it. And there were set there six waterpots of stone, after the manner of the purifying of the Jews, containing two or three firkins apiece."*

Figuratively and spiritually speaking, the third day represents the spirit man, the second day represents the soul of man, and the first day represents the natural man. We must understand that this is the make up of man—spirit, soul, and body. Here are some more keys.

Key #1 (Verse 1)

This is the third day, (representing having dealt with the flesh and the mind), that period after we surpass religion and self. It literally takes some people three days or more to get in touch with the spirit man and to contact God. When this occurs, a joining together of the Spirit of God, and the spirit of man takes place. The birth of the anointing and spirit of truth becomes apparent through prayer, repentance, and humility.

24

Key #2 (Verse 2)

True worship takes place when the representation of heaven (Jesus or the Holy Spirit) and earth's representation (disciples or the soul) meet up together for the same purpose (in this case, the purpose is to produce true worship).

Key #3 (Verse 3)

They needed worship, which is typical of the need for wine or the need for the Holy Spirit. I am sure they had wine, initially, they just needed new wine.

Key #4 (Verse 4)

Timing is critical. The spirit has a special hour and time to give us true worship. We must tarry until He invites us into His presence. As we draw nigh to Him, He will draw nigh to us.

Key #5 (Verse 5)

We must be attentive to the voice of the Spirit and be obedient as well. In essence, true worship is doing, saying, and responding to heaven in the way we are spiritually prompted to respond.

Key #6 (Verse 6)

We must be willing vessels with a desire to be purified. The Jewish manner of purification was to continually pour fresh water into a waterpot until it overflowed. This was a natural form of washing away of impurities. It is the same for us, as we continually receive the washing and cleansing power of the water of the word of God washing over our soul. Why? Simply, the body does what the mind tells it.

Now, let us look further into this text for more prophetic insights.

II. Receiving the Spirit of Worship
John Chapter Two, verses 7-12

"Jesus saith unto them, Fill the waterpots with water. And they filled them up to the brim. And he saith unto them, Draw out now, and bear unto the governor of the feast. And they bare it. When the ruler of the feast had tasted the water that was made wine, and knew not whence it was: (but the servants which drew the water knew;) the governor of the feast called the bridegroom, And saith unto him, Every man at the beginning doth set forth good wine; and when men have well drunk, then that which is worse: but thou hast kept the good wine until now. This beginning of miracles did Jesus in Cana of Galilee, and manifested forth his glory; and his disciples believed on him. After this he went down to Capernaum, he, and his mother, and his brethren, and his disciples: and they continued there not many days."

Key #7 (Verse 7)

Praise is the act that starts the flow of the infilling of the spirit of worship. We must praise God with all of our strength. Once we have given our human efforts to our limits, then the Spirit floods our spirit to create the best worship.

Key #8 (Verse 8)

We place a greater demand on heaven by pouring out our hearts in thanksgiving to Jesus Christ. When heaven senses that we are sincere in heart and pure in motives, we are touched and transformed from the inside out - from water to new wine.

Key #9 (Verses 9-10)

When Jesus Christ discerns that the atmosphere is ready to receive His presence (after he has tasted of the sweet savors of thanksgiving and sacrificial praise) then, He comes and fills us with His anointing to worship. The best songs or worship comes after we have spent our natural resources.

Key #10 (Verse 11)

This prepares the atmosphere for deliverance, miracles and healings. The glory of God is ready to be manifested and the faith of the believer is charged to receive the more of Jesus via the preaching of the word. (Note that this was Jesus' first visit to Cana as previously mentioned in Chapter Two, however, both visitations had an element of worship and its results.

Key #11 (Verse 12)

Jesus and worship will not be manifested where there is ignorance of and an unwillingness for His presence. The visit will always be very brief. Many believers miss true worship moments because we are more attentive to the under-shepherd – the pastor, than to the Chief Shepherd – Jesus. They have become idol worshippers. We should honor our leaders, but only Jesus is to be worshipped.

Now, let us view some radical outcomes of true worship.

III. The Radical Results of Worship
John Chapter Two, verses 13– 25

"And the Jews' Passover was at hand, and Jesus went up to Jerusalem, And found him in the temple those that sold oxen and sheep and doves, and the changers of money sitting: And when he had made a scourge of small cords, he drove them all out of the temple, and the

sheep, and the oxen; and poured out the changers' money, and overthrew the tables; And said unto them that sold doves, Take these things hence; make not my Father's house a house of merchandise. And his disciples remembered that it was written, The zeal of thine house hath eaten me up. Then answered the Jews and said unto Him, What sign shewest thou unto us, seeing that thou doest these things? Jesus answered and said unto them, Destroy this temple, and in three days I will raise it up. Then said the Jews, Forty and six years was this temple in building, and wilt thou rear it up in three days? But he spake of the temple of his body. When therefore he was risen from the dead, his disciples remembered that he had said this unto them; and they believed the scripture, and the word which Jesus had said. Now when he was in Jerusalem at the Passover, in the feast day, many believed in his name, when they saw the miracles which he did. But Jesus did not commit himself unto them, because he knew all men, And indeed not that any should testify of man: for he knew what was in man."

Key #12 (Verse 13)

In true worship, as we continually remember the previous events and acts of deliverance, we will become radically affected by the desire to invite Jesus into our midst to reign and rule. True worship always goes upward. Capernaum was downward but Jerusalem was upward. Jesus dwells where worship is upward.

28

Key #13 (Verse 14)

Oftentimes people come to the place of prayer and praise for everything but the right things. These pervert the place of worship and cause pockets, cracks, and breaches for demonic activity to operate in. Most people come to the temple to sit and to be entertained rather than to give glory to God and receive grace from God.

Key #14 (Verse 15)

Radical praise will silence the voice of demons and paralyze the enemy. Radical worship or His fullest glory-presence comes after radical praise. Most times, we like Jesus, have to enter into spiritual warfare and an act of praise before we can enter into the spirit of worship.

Key #15 (Verse 16)

The voice of praise and prayer will reaffirm to the Lord that His presence is welcome in the house. Praise and worship displaces the devil and all demonic activity.

Key #16 (Verses 17-18)

The enemy will always oppose and seek to discourage true praise and worship because it always brings positive results. Remember that you are not trying to impress or prove Jesus to anyone. His liberty and presence, which is part of His spirit, will speak for Himself.

Key #17 (Verse 19)

Real worship cannot be defeated by the tactics or talk of the enemy nor by religion. True worship puts you into another dimension that non-worshippers cannot go into.

Key #18 (Verses 20-22)

True worship places you into 3-D mode, the third dimension, or the spirit realm (where there is prophetic utterance, revelation knowledge and spiritual discernment) which others do not understand. You are the temple that He indwells.

Key #19 (Verse 23)

True worship increases our faith and our supernatural ability. Jesus was, and is, the greatest worshipper ever known. Although He is our great High Priest, He sits at the right hand of the Father to make intercession for us. Whenever we call on His name, we literally ask Him to remind the Father that He is our offering, our praise, and our worship connection.

Key #20 (Verses 24-25)

True worship leaves you empowered and humbled and with a greater desire to worship the Lord of lords and the King of kings. Although Jesus was God in the flesh, He wanted no glory for Himself; rather, He gave glory to the Father in heaven. Keep the glory focused on the Father and not us humans, the fallen.

Now that we have established a taste for worship, let us remember that it's not always easy to just worship. However, the test for true worshippers comes into question when we are challenged by satan to abandon our lifestyle of worship. Satan's kingdom of darkness cannot stand to hear true worship, so it mounts attacks against every true worshipper, every worshipping church, and every worshipping home.

Are you under attack in your church? Are you under attack on your job? Are you under attack in your city? Are you under attack at home?

Perhaps, it's because you are a true worshipper. So what do you do now? I'll tell you –Just worship – pump up the volume on your praise and worship!

JUST WORSHIP KEY

The best songs, or worship, comes after we have spent our natural resources. This is when we receive the Lord's song. It's a tehillah song; a song of the Spirit.

Chapter Four

BECOMING A WARRIOR IN WORSHIP

"Therefore rejoice, ye heavens, and ye that dwell in them. Woe to the inhabiters of the earth and of the sea; for the devil is come down unto you, having great wrath, because he knoweth that he hath but a short time" (Revelation 12:12).

The twelfth Chapter of the book of Revelation gives us a vivid picture of what took place in the heavenlies before satan and his angels were evicted from their first estate. I am a certified history teacher, by training, and I would not claim to be totally accurate on the timeline of the text of Revelation Chapter 12. However, it is apparent and widely accepted among bible scholars to be the warfare between Michael-the Archangel, and satan-the once anointed cherub, and his fallen kingdom.

The story is fairly simple as it chronicles how satan decided to rebel against God. He sought to exalt his own throne above the throne of God. The warrior Archangel, Michael, evicted him along with his followers – fallen angels.

It goes on to say that he seeks to get revenge on God for his demotion by getting at His beloved creation, especially the inhabiters of the earth, humans. All of this retribution is taking place at a fast pace because the devil knows that his time is short. This is why we experience so many difficulties, delays, detours, distractions, and discouragements on our journey in serving the Lord.

It is satan's goal to get our focus off of worshipping the true King of kings and Lord of lords, and instead, focus on speaking about what he is trying to do to keep us from serving God.

Since I am a visual learner, I am also inclined to be a visual-audio teacher. Examine if you will the following graphic organizer in the format of a Venn diagram. (A Venn diagram helps us to see the correlation between one or more dynamics of a relationship. It is often used in mathematics.) It attempts to elucidate the concept of worship in spirit and truth.

WORSHIP

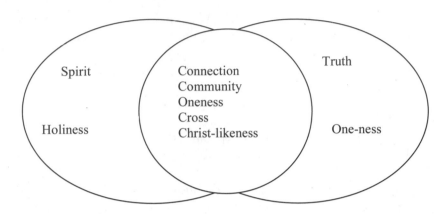

DEFAULT BY WILL

I should first mention that the ultimate goal of all acts of worship is to bring glory to God and to conform us more to the image and character of Christ. Christ-likeness is the desired result of worship. Worship, whether in the form of:

- tithing
- communion
- praise and worship
- baptism, or
- preaching

always points us to Christ-likeness. We are sought by God to worship Him in spirit and in truth. Within these two elements are the attributes of holiness and oneness or singleness.

The book of James refers to God as having no variableness or shadow of turning (James 1:17). In short, if it's of God, it's of truth. Moreover, the power of the Holy Spirit permits us to be holy in relating to God and the power of the word helps us to be single-minded and not having two opposing promises to trust in. This, in essence, is what's termed a compromise.

So the question would then be what is it that breaks in on and fights against the goal or desired results of worship? It is the direct difficulties designed by satan to delay, detour, distract, and discourage everyone, particularly, true worshipers from freely worshipping God.

Therefore when we worship in spirit and in truth, invariably we are being transformed from our carnal nature to being conformed to the image and character of God. We learn how to become better connected, more in community to the body of Christ, our family, and the world, more conscious of the power and purpose of covenant and how to gracefully endure and bear our cross without complaining. These different ingredients blend together to exemplify our Christ-likeness. This is what I call the art of being, according to John 1:12. Worship helps us to become sons and daughters of God.

When we receive the Spirit of Christ, He gives us the power to become the sons of God. Look closely, it says sons. That denotes a level of maturity, unlike that of a child of God, who is still immature and carnal. To be quite honest with you there are only two times or in two instances when we should worship the Lord, one is when we want to and secondly, when we don't want to.

In summation, what I am trying to show in the Venn diagram about the concept of worship is that spirit and truth are given to us by God as a whole, or as a two-sided coin, if you understand that better. It carry along with it spirit and holiness on one side, and truth and oneness, or unity, on the other side. When we receive God's Spirit, we essentially possess His holiness to a degree. Likewise, when we receive His truth, we also potentially have the ability to walk in oneness or in His unity and love. When we truly tap into real worship, it produces the characteristics of connection, community, oneness with the body of Christ, our family, and our community. This is not oneness with sin or sinners, outside of the body of Christ, but a Phileo (brotherly love) or Christian type of love for humanity. Christians really should be humble and meek, like Christ. It is our self-centeredness or sin that stops this from taking place freely. Therefore, to get us to deliberately act in accordance to His will, to serve and worship Him, we are given a cross to bear daily. Why?

It is the cross that we bear that brings out this Christ-likeness. Remember, I said in earlier chapters that we should worship in spite of our cross. Why? Because this is what brings about Christ-likeness.

Whenever we forfeit or default at worship, it is by will or our choice. Oftentimes it takes conflict or warfare to produce true worship.

I have heard some use the argument of Apostle Paul's explanation in Roman's Chapter Seven concerning the war of the flesh against the spirit, and how they are always in conflict and in counter distinction of one another, erroneously. Many utilize this text for justification to be weak and carnal. This is not what this text is saying at all. Let's take a closer look at it.

I want to lift up specific verses and bring some clarity to the intrinsic passion of Paul's resolution as it relates to salvation and worship.

The main point I want to make is that salvation and worshipping in spirit and truth are acts of the human will or the soul seat of the spiritual man:

- God does not save us against our will to be saved.
- God does not make us worship Him beyond our will to worship Him.

David says it like this:

> *"I will bless the Lord at all times; His praises shall continually be in my mouth" (Psalm 34:1).*

David willed to bless the Lord. It is always our choice to choose to worship or to continue to confess the word of God with our mouth, believe in our minds or soul, and then by faith receive in our spirit the promises of salvation. This is why the book of James tells us to receive the engrafted word of God which is able to save our souls (James 1:21).

This is the very thing that causes satan and his demons to get upset. The fact that in spite of all the difficulties, distractions, discouragements, delays, and detours, he is permitted by God to design to work against us; we remain steadfast in our will to praise and worship and to love God Almighty (Romans 8:22-39):

- We who were created a little lower (in a different class) than angels;
- We who have never been where angels have;

- We who are the broken, fallen, and redeemed, and who love not our lives unto death, still have praise and worship for our Lord of lords.

This terrifies satan and silences demons. I know I sidetracked my argument on Paul-*but I needed to preach a little bit.*

The devil and his fallen kingdom lost their first estates, now they seek to inhabit praising, worshipping, reverencing, God-conscious humans – the current real estates. We are God's prized property. Actually, in God's eyesight, we are the real estate that houses His praise in which glory and honor to Him reside in. Inside of every human being is the potential to silence and put to shame the voice of demons by their praise and worship in spirit and in truth. Once we accept Jesus Christ as Lord of our lives and our spirit man is regenerated, we become a part of a new spiritual generation whose destiny is to worship in spirit and in truth. Shout glory to God!

Now that I've said that, I'm back! I promise to deal with the context of the book of Romans Chapter seven, but I felt the redirection of the Holy Spirit to deal with what I just stated above.

First, I want to focus on the central point of my argument and that is, although the Apostle Paul is struggling with his carnal nature, he is a regenerated, born-again, and spirit filled Christian. In direct opposition of this thesis is the antithesis that an unregenerated, unbeliever and sinner is not subject to the voice, ways or will of God (Romans 7:5-9). They do not know God. They are not reconciled to, or in relationship with, God.

Having stated that, let us look at some parts of the text.

> *"For we know that the law is spiritual: but I am carnal, sold under sin. For that which I do I allow not: for what I would, that do I not; but what I hate, that do I. If then I do that which I would not, I consent unto the law that it is good. Now then it is no more I that do it, but sin that dwelleth in me. For I know that in me (that is, in my flesh) dwelleth no good thing: for to will is present with me; but how to perform that which is good I find not. For the good that I would I do not: but the evil which I would not, that I do. Now if I do*

that I would not, it is no more I that do it, but sin that dwelleth in me. I find then a law, that, when I would do good, evil is present with me. For I delight in the law of God after the inward man: but I see another law in my members, warring against the law of my mind, and bringing me into captivity to the law of sin which is in my members. O wretched man that I am! Who shall deliver me from the body of this death? I thank God through Jesus Christ our Lord. So then with the mind I myself serve the law of God; but with the flesh the law of sin" (Romans 7:14-25).

If I were not a practicing believer of the power, presence, and purpose of Jesus Christ, I would think that Apostle Paul was influenced by some of the great philosophers of the past and the present day. He is very eloquent in this presentation in dealing with the art of inductive and deductive reasoning and the art of negations. However, to the true believer, this is not just philosophical ponderance, rather it is more reality than many of us would admit. Therefore, I just want to make a few observations because this entire text would easily provide preaching material for an entire year.

We should immediately notice that Paul's usage of the personal pronoun "I" twenty seven times from verses fourteen through twenty-five is a strong indication of the implied act of His will. Both the phrases, "What I would" and "when I would" are equal to the negations of "I do that I would not" and "for that which I do I allow not." In each phrase grouping, he is talking about the power of choice given to every physically and mentally healthy individual. We have the ability to choose to worship, or not.

Secondly, he makes the counter-distinction of the law of God after the inward man or the law of the spirit of life in Christ Jesus from the law of the flesh or the law of sin and death. I strongly believe that the law of sin and death has a lot to do with what the scripture refers to regarding the mystery of iniquity in II Thessalonians 2:1-13. I believe that satan and demons have power to show forth their power as we (humans) yield our physical body and mind to him and his seducing spirits. It is very subtle. We do not outright say 'satan I am willing to be disobedient to God along with you', but we do yield to the workings of the flesh and his kingdom by surprise attacks. He cunningly attacks when we are weak and not sober or vigilant. I placed surprise attacks that are devised by the enemy into two different categories with four sources each. I don't want to take too much time in explaining them, but I will touch on them briefly. Surprise attacks from the devil come from:

- **the crowd**
- **carnal people**
- **co-workers and**
- **companions**

This is the first assault group. The crowd is people in general or society at large. Carnal people are non-believers and immature believers we do not necessarily hang out with, but we often come in contact with them. If the first two do not weaken us enough, then satan utilizes our co-workers; the folks on the job; the ones we must see and interact with almost on a daily basis. Maybe you are being attacked right now through an ungodly, foul-mouthed supervisor who just curses to boil your blood. Don't quit the job like the devil wants you to, rather, just go into the bathroom and worship. That's right, take a worship break in the corner and just worship. When you return everyone will smell the sweet aroma of worship instead of a frustrated, faulting person. The last attack is a real challenge because it's your companion, or spouse. During the time of attack you can't live around this person without learning how to tap into heaven for yourself. Sometimes it's you and other times it's your spouse. The devil doesn't care who it is, he just wants to cause strife and stop worship and the anointing.

The next group that the devil uses consists of:

- **foes**
- **friends**
- **family, and**
- **familiar-spirits**

We can easily, sooner or later, recognize our foes. They are always blocking our progress. However, many of us do not realize that sometimes there comes a time when our friends are tools of the enemy or when we simply outgrow them and should limit our contact with them. Later, they may grow too or maybe not. Perhaps you will remain friends or possibly not. God knows and when He believes it's time to tell you what to do, He will tell you. I guess the biggest hindrances to our crosswalk can come from the ones we love the most – our family. We see this principle being played out in many lives in scripture, within the examples of Abraham, Gideon and Jesus. Family will stop you from serving God, if you let them. Don't let them. Love them, but don't let them stop your divine destiny.

Finally, there are familiar spirits. They are those evil spirits that have been with us for so long that we welcome them as family. You know, like lust, fear, uncleanness, lying, perversion, divination, and idolatry, just to mention a few. These are the things that creep up on us and attach themselves onto our flesh to weaken us and to keep us weak. They are seemingly ever present. Even after three and four weeks of Holy Convocation and a hot, fiery deliverance service, they are assisted by one glance at a book, or a television show, or by the innocent listening of a CD or a certain radio station. It is what Paul meant by saying evil is always present, even when I want to do good. This, I believe, is a part of the mystery of iniquity. That is, the flesh will always be a point of entry and attack for and from the powers of darkness. However, the victory comes as we apply our will to obey God's word and by the indwelling power of the Holy Spirit.

There can be no true worship without true obedience. When this happens, the power of the Holy Spirit quickens or makes living our dead bodies. This is quintessential to what the bible refers to as the mystery of Godliness. (I Timothy 3:16). The law of sin and death governs our flesh, and it's at enmity with God. But, our inward spirit is governed by the indwelling power of the Holy Spirit, and it possesses that intrinsic power to put to death the deeds of the flesh and arise in power to obey the word of God. (Romans 8:5-14). Therefore, when we persevere to obey God, we become disciples of Christ or disciplined in the things of Godliness. We become sons rather than mere immature children. This is the beginning mindset of a warrior in worship. It is our task, under the great commission, to make disciples, (Matthew 28:19-20), and not just be large congregations with crowds of carnal people. True Christians are committed to the cause of Christ.

Finally, I want to draw your attention to these phrases found in Romans 8:28, 35 and 37, "to them that love God," "from the love of

Christ" and "through him that loved us." I encourage you to read Romans Chapters Seven and Eight as one, in its entirety, to really comprehend what the Spirit is saying. All of these verses deal with the dynamics of love - the agape or God kind of love. This again is not to strengthen the argument of a free ride to weakness and carnality as some eternal salvation doctrine believers believe. We must look not just at interpretation of scripture, but also at application. However, if our interpretation is in error, surely our application will be as well.

Please notice that Paul says, "to them that love God." This means to love Him by obeying His word. This is how Jesus explained it (John 14:24). Many of us love God the way we interpret love, yet Jesus says, not so, and that it is impossible to love God without seeking or willing to obey His word. If we can do wrong and it never convicts us, then something is wrong. You cannot say I love the Lord with all my heart and never read His word, never go to bible study and never show any fruit of the spirit. (Galatians 5:22-25). These are not the character traits of one who loves God. Then, some believe that nothing can separate us from the love of Christ. I believe that the only thing that can separate us from Christ's love is us. We choose to love Him the way His word admonishes us to do. If Judas never loved Jesus, then our teaching on there being twelve disciples is historically in error. I think Judas was a disciple.

I am also reminded of the story of Esau who chose to sell his birthright to his brother, Jacob, for something for the flesh, and though he sought God with tears and repentance, there was not a place for him to return to – that once assigned place. I believe God loves us to the end, and if we want the will of God done in our life, He will help us reach that predestined place. But, on the other hand, it is God's decision to cancel our assigned destiny because of our own disobedience or rebellion. We've seen it time and time again – someone being used mightily by God and because they refuse to heed Godly correction, they're chastened of the Lord. They still refuse to humble themselves; they go on a slide on the wild side and get caught on the outside.

It is only then they are allowed by God's gracious mercy to repent and come back to Him, because He remembers our labors of love toward Him. Some do and others don't. Remember, God judges all unconfessed sin. This is why I believe we can easily get so far away from God's presence because after we have been saved for a long time, we believe that we don't have to confess sin nor repent anymore. We have become so familiar with the move of God, and we think we are equal with God. Form will never replace God's power; it is His power and presence which gives us victory over the flesh.

Don't be deceived, God is not mocked. The point that I want you to see is that we are in a spiritual warfare and that satan is fighting to win. To always worship is a choice of the individual's will. If we want to show our love for God in spite of the warfare, God will shed His love abroad in our heart by the Holy Spirit, which will cause our faith to work. If we will to worship in spirit and in truth, He will guide us in this too. Paul says it best in Romans Chapter nine.

"I say the truth in Christ, I lie not, my conscience also bearing me witness in the Holy Ghost" (Romans 9:1). As the Venn diagram illustrates, the only time we don't show true worship to God is by default of our own will. Whether in seasons of calm or conflict, we must learn that we are created to worship God.

I talked to you about the spiritual dynamics of becoming a warrior in worship. In the next Chapter, I want to define for you who I believe an effective warrior in worship is and some attributes and elements which are also very critical for warriors in worship to possess and comprehend.

JUST WORSHIP KEY

Remember, the battle belongs to the Lord. Stand up and give Him a shout of praise for the battle belongs to the Lord!!!

Chapter Five

WARRIORS IN WORSHIP

"And after these things I heard a great voice of much people in heaven, saying, Alleluia; salvation, and glory, and honour, and power, unto the Lord our God... And I saw heaven opened, and behold a white horse; and he that sat upon him was called faithful and true, and in righteousness he doth judge and make war" (Revelation 19:1,11).

For those of you who are bible scholars, I want you to know that I know that the book of Revelation is about the Revelation of Jesus Christ. It is divided into three components in terms of a timeline: (1) that which was; (2) that which is; and (3) that which is to come. I also understand that the testimony of Jesus is the spirit of prophecy. Revelation speaks of who Jesus was as a child, who Jesus was as a suffering servant, who Jesus is as a resurrected King and Lord, and who Jesus will be in the New Jerusalem. In order to get a better picture of what I am going to highlight in this chapter, I want to visit the story of Jesus' triumphant entry into Jerusalem almost three thousand Jewish years ago.

Jesus showed us a key principle as it relates to spiritual warfare and worship in Matthew the twenty-first chapter. In the beginning of the chapter, He makes His triumphal entry into the city of worship and peace in the shadow of great praise. It is then that others in the city inquire of Him and seek to know Him.

In the twelfth verse, we find Jesus cleansing, or warring, in the temple (church) with the moneychangers and the seat of them that sold doves (sacrifices to be offered to God for His blessings or, the anointing). He says "It is written, my house shall be called a house of prayer; but ye have made it a den of thieves." This looks very much like our day. Some people have only the motive to self-profit off of the church, rather than to properly steward their anointing to maximize the extent of their effectiveness and reach into the great end time harvest of souls. This is what eternal purpose is all about. What we gain here will not ultimately profit us, rather it is what we present to Jesus, eternally. The rest is mere stubble and hay, which will be burned when tried.

After this incident, great healings and deliverances took place. I believe that the new millennium church will experience more healings and deliverances when we get worship right. The religious people and satan, of course, were displeased that everyone was praising Jesus, the King. But He simply responded in verse sixteen with this scripture: "And said unto Him (Jesus), hearest thou what these say? And Jesus saith unto them, yea; have ye never read, out of the mouth of babes and sucklings thou hast perfected praise?" (Matthew 21:26). This verse ties in with Psalm 8:1-2.

> *"O LORD our Lord, how excellent is thy Name in all the earth! Who hast set thy Glory above the heavens. Out of the mouth of babes and sucklings hast thou ordained strength because of thine enemies, that thou mightest still the enemy and the avenger."*

The point I want to make is that God is a man of war. We see this played out time and time again in the scriptures, especially in the Psalms, in prayers of His servants, and through the prophetic voices of His prophets. In the first two verses of Chapter 144 of the Psalms, we see King David being used as a prophetic voice. He says, God teaches him to war with his fingers and hands. How does the Lord accomplish this task? We find it in the ninth verse when David declares that upon a psaltery and an instrument of ten strings will I sing praises unto thee. A clear demonstration of this was displayed by David, when he played skillfully and ministered deliverance to King Saul through the strings of his harp (I Samuel 16:14-23). David was a true warrior in worship. This is why David was promoted in the kingdom over his brothers. Why? He celebrated Jesus. If you celebrate Him, you will be elevated in life. God in His songs, the Lord's song, is a man of war.

One purpose of a warrior in worship is to show forth goodness because warring worship liberates the oppressed. Further allow me to define the following questions:

- What is the believer's role as a warrior in worship?
- Who is a warrior in worship?

I believe that there are some basic characteristics of those I have termed, "Warriors in Worship." However, I need to lay a strong foundation based on some key principles and relationships within the scriptures before I give them to you.

I strongly believe the essential elements of receiving the revelation of Warriors in Worship is found in the relationships and principles of the earthly Jesus Christ and the resurrected Jesus Christ. These two descriptions are found in the New Testament in the gospels concerning His triumphal entry, and the other is found in the context of Revelation Chapter 19 verses 1 and 11. In the gospels, He is a humble king, riding a donkey, which is typical of a peaceful Jesus Christ. He was praised by some and despised by others, yet He did not respond to their reactions to Him. He just existed in the reality that the Kingship in Him was worthy of worship. However, there is a counter-distinction in Revelation 19. Worship is given to Him in the heavens but He is dressed in blood stained war clothes, and on His commanding white horse, typical of a general. In verse eleven, it says "He doth judge and make war."

Simply put, we as believers in Christ (we are the body), Christ is the head of the body of Christ on earth. Therefore, we have the role of conducting spiritual warfare through praise and worship in the earth. What He decreed in His word we must declare in the earth, and the host of heaven demonstrates it in the heavenlies and the earth. What is our assignment or role as warriors in worship? We have been given the task to host and invite others to a praise and worship festival, a triumphant celebration, and to set the stage and atmosphere for the M.I.P. (Most Important Person) the Lord of Hosts – Jesus Christ. We are mere hosts for Him. Who is a warrior in worship?

Worship is always measured in degrees of glory, like the songs of degrees in the divisions of Psalms. Remember that we always ascend up to the heavenlies, like the Hebrew songs of the Old Testament ascend in temple worship.

One day during my daily devotion, I asked God to teach me how to worship Him. Ironically, while in a wilderness experience, a season of warfare, God taught me about true worship. It was there where I began to sing and articulate new prayers and prophetic words into songs and melodies. Much to my surprise (I am not a skilled singer) it created a majestic atmosphere, which resonated a sense of a royal procession.

Just like it is recorded in the text, this is exactly what had taken place in the heavenlies in my wilderness days. The true and only potentate had come to be enthroned and to inhabit the praises of His people. In His showing up He prepared a feast of peace, love, joy, faith, and many other things for me in the presence of my enemies.

I can better explain this awesome experience by giving you a word picture. Imagine that Ross Perot or Bill Gates, or any other billionaire had extended to you a personal invitation to their Mediterranean Sea-docked, one hundred foot, luxury yacht. More than one thousand of their dearest friends, including yourself, are airlifted to the yacht by a custom-built helicopter. When you arrive on the yacht, you are ushered into a special dressing room where you are bathed and given an Egyptian mummy wrap in soothing massage oils. After this, you are furnished with a tuxedo or beautiful gown, and shoes. There is a hair stylist on the yacht who grooms your hair for you. Then, you are ushered onto the main deck of the yacht where there is the best food and drinks money can buy. Ostensibly, the yacht is covered with paid hosts and hostesses. They are greeting the invites for the purpose of making each individual feel special, before the host shows up.

Already elated and honored, the paid hosts and hostesses give everyone a one-carat diamond pendant. Then, all of a sudden, the airspace above the yacht is surrounded with the sound of a custom made jet that hovers over the main deck and lowers a ladder onto the luxury sea vessel. To everyone's surprise, but much anticipation, guess who comes out of the jet cockpit? None other than the host. Everyone is attempting, to the best of their ability, to praise and thank the host for providing them with such a stupendous and lavish evening.

This scenario is as near to accurate a word picture of an indescribable occurrence of what the bible refers to, (and what I experienced in the sense that I felt like royalty), when it speaks of the Lord of Host being revealed. Yes, the angelic hosts are always doing their best to represent the strength, the grace, and the love of God in most situations involving the believer; however, every now and then, the Lord of the Host stops by, personally, to handle things Himself. And, when the Lord of Host shows up, things are much greater than ever. Worship and praise in song is, for sure, one of those times He alone inhabits the praise of His people. He stops by and handles things Himself. I can remember vividly, He made this a glorious and rapturous experience for me. It seemed as if I was the only person in the world that mattered. Of course, this is not true; He loves all mankind. It just seemed like that to me.

I believe that there is a remnant of worshippers in the Body of Christ who have an awesome responsibility of being Warriors in Worship through music, poems or psalms, prayers and prophetic voices, and to change environments and cities, dethrone principalities and powers, to provide comfort to the discomforted and guidance to the dazed and confused wanderers. They will, among other things, be channels of rescue, reconciliation, and renewal for the kingdom of God. Take this time to seek the face of God. You may be one of the warriors in worship God is seeking. When we have received the challenge of this task, we will find that the results will be the empowerment of lives for His kingdom. It is not a hit or miss proposition, nor is it some kind of serendipitous event, but rather it is an intentional and fully persuasive view that we must embrace.

I know, and have come to believe, by practical experience as well as by revelation, that this is a divine and ageless principle. God has, with purpose, given us a weapon that is mighty, a weapon that is living, and powerful, and sharper than any two-edged sword, piercing even to the dividing asunder of soul and spirit, and of the joints and marrow, and is a discerner of the thoughts and intents of the heart – His word and the name and covenant of His son Jesus. (Hebrew 4:12). This weapon is not only to be utilized by the preacher in his text, but it is also to be used by the singer, the songwriter, the producer, and the musician through psalms, prayers, and prophetic voices in songs and in worship.

I personally believe that comfort, guidance, and empowerment comes from prophetic worship and fresh Spirit songs. This is what poems, prayers, and prophetic voices in the songs of the Lord should achieve, in every age. Yet, we have lost some of that vision in this hour to accomplish this goal. Undoubtedly, with the church's position of compromise, we have lost something in our ability to ascend into the presence of God, and to open the door for others. Nevertheless, I believe a new glory is coming in the realm of psalms, prayers, and prophetic voices – the Lord's songs. God always requires confession and repentance before restoration. Lord, I confess for the Body of Christ, and for my brothers and sisters in the dark, to these truths. I stand in the gap. I believe if we, the Body of Christ, songwriters,

47

:ists, performers, producers, and the like, would confess that we have deed, and in spirit, missed it, God's mercy would kick in.

We must confess that we have not discerned God's real purpose for 1aring our gifts of music, lyrics, prayers, and prophetic voices because /e have not sought, nor understood their role in bringing in His ▸resence. Then, He would restore us and release a new wave of His glory. In addition, we must realize that because of our past compromising position, many have also lost track of their souls by cross mixing the message of the cross with untrue and mere emotionally packaged man-made, sensualistic inspired lyrics. Lyrics are as powerfully packed as a Holy Spirit inspired sermon. We are sending dangerous and erroneous messages to our youth by embracing crossover artists without telling them the difference between a Christian witness and a professional singer. Therefore, sin, self, and satan are seemingly abounding in our youth culture and in our land today. But God wants to begin to redirect the pathways of our souls into direct access, tracks into the very presence of God. He wants to direct us into the portals of empowerment by His glory.

When we reach this plateau in our comprehension, that the purpose of psalms, prayers, and prophetic voices in songs is to intentionally serve to reestablish the divine kingdom order of the throne of God in the earth, we will see, know, and begin to take our place as warriors in worship. Then, kingdom praise in the earth realm will resound in the hearts and souls of men and the greatest move of the Holy Spirit will declare the Lordship of Jesus Christ as the ultimate poem, psalmist warrior, intercessor, and prophetic voice in the universe. Hear what the Spirit says to the church:

The battle is over
And the victory has been won
All hail, King Emmanuel
All praises to the son
Let us shout with a voice of triumph
Worthy is our Lord
With extended hands of thanksgiving
All on one accord
All hail, King Jesus
Reign Emmanuel

All hail, king mighty in battle
He forever reigns on the throne.

This prophetic song is one that I sing many times before I go into a spiritual battle. Why? Because we can do what Jesus has already done. I also believe that in order to maintain, sustain, and make gains, we must learn to seek and pursue the presence of God with an unrelenting passion through praise and worship, prayer and proclaiming the power of God which is the word of God. We will find that we will have experiences with the re-visitation of His glory - Jesus Christ, the Anointed one, the Prince of Peace, the Joy of Our Salvation, and our Healer more frequently.

We must begin to tap into the spirit realm and learn how to gain immediate access to comfort, guidance, and empowerment for others and ourselves. When we tap into His presence, we will find His peace, prosperity, and His creative power.

In the next Chapter, I want to highlight some thoughts about the passion of true worship. Worship is no less than dynamite.

JUST WORSHIP KEY

If you celebrate Him, you will be elevated in life.

Chapter Six

WORSHIP IS LIKE DYNAMITE

"God hath spoken once; twice have I heard this, that power belongs to God" (Psalm 62:11).

Man is forever seeking to understand the wonders of God's creation. Once He permits us to comprehend certain things in His creation, such as power in the forces of nature and man-made concepts of powerful forces, such as bombs and dynamite, many times we utilize it and abuse it. There are a lot of things in the earth that are neutral, but when fallen men and women get a hold of anything, it has the potential to be used for evil rather than good.

Have you ever wondered why music is such a powerful tool? I have, and I want to make the following observations as it relates to the spirit realm and worship.

Music can be, and should be, used as a mighty spiritual weapon. Most musicians are so into themselves, they cannot discern the spiritual needs of others. I believe that there is a song, a note, a key, or a praise for every oppression and possession of the kingdom of darkness. Remember, before satan and a third of the angelic hosts fell, they used to sing, praise, hit keys and notes, while offering worship to God. I also believe that in their fall, their ability to love and to function in those same songs, notes, keys, and praise was lost. The only thing different about this loss is that they do not want to find what they lost. It's like a deviant minded person taking a bomb and placing it in a black duffel bag and sitting it next to a crowded store he intended to blow up. He leaves the duffel bag and briskly walks away. Some unsuspecting person runs behind him, quickly, to return what they perceive to be a lost or forgotten bag. Not knowing the contents of the duffel bag, they return it to the demented man and shortly thereafter, the bomb explodes.

I can imagine that even before the bomb exploded, the man went through a very discomforting feeling. Why? Because he tried his hardest to get away from the bag and bomb, knowing its capability. He knows that the contents of the duffel bag are explosive and damaging. This is how satan and his kingdom are. Satan and demons are irked when we sing and praise, and musicians play certain keys and notes skillfully on their instruments. True worship and passionate prayer is an explosive to demons that has a destructive force in their kingdom. Real worship reminds them of the majestic and enthroned Lordship of Jesus Christ. It reminds them of what they left behind. They can't stand to hear that sound coming from humans – who are not even in their created class. We were created a little lower than the angels. (Psalm 8:4-6).

Real passionate worship has the capability of bringing with it victory in spiritual battles. Sometimes the battles in the spiritual realm are heavy and intense, and at other times light and easy. They are not that way for Jesus, but for us. Therefore, there is really no room to get caught up in pride. We never get the full force of the battle, but we do experience that part of Christ's suffering being birthed in us. And we sooner or later learned that the route to total victory and the anointing is through the blood, the fire, and the water. I deal more in-depth with this concept in a future chapter. This is a warrior in worship concept.

In this Warrior in Worship principle and relationship, Jesus is no longer the meek lamb on a donkey. He is a man of war. He is the exalted warring warrior, watching over His word, to perform it. He calls and commands; we confess it and He confirms it. (Hebrews 2:3-4, 12).

> "How shall we escape, if we neglect so great salvation; which at the first began to be spoken by the Lord, and was confirmed unto us by them that heard him; God also bearing them witness, both with signs and wonders, and with divers miracles, and gifts of the Holy Ghost, according to His own will? Saying, I will declare thy name [in His name we find His covenant of salvation] unto my brethren, in the midst of the church will I sing praise unto thee."

You may be wondering what I am trying to say. Well first, remember, they that call on the name of the Lord shall be saved. Secondly, also remember that God judges our confession of praise, worship, and prophecy. Then, He goes before us to wage war. He leads and commands an angelic host, who hearken to the voice of His saints singing His word in worship.

The text portrays this dynamic and holy exchange; God singing the praises of Jesus in the midst of the church through us, His Body. The Lord's song is sung directly by Jesus because its source is from the Holy Spirit.

If you note in Revelation Chapter 19, Jesus' only vesture was dipped in blood. This is not true of the armies in heaven, or the saints who were dressed in white linen. It is also noteworthy, and vital, to know that some spiritual battles, as in the case with end time battles, are neither for the angels, nor for the saints, but rather these battles belong to the Lord. He will perform His word and bring to pass His promises. Jesus is not like the earthly general who commands from the protected back base. He goes before us and conquers. All we're to do is send up high praises and quote the word at His command.

It is satan's desire for us to default in worship by cunningly and deceptively getting us to be ungrateful in attitude, to murmur and complain, to openly be disobedient, and to act in disbelief. But as a warrior in worship, we are on divine assignment. We have a threefold mandate. First, we are to prophetically proclaim the devil's defeat and destruction in every circumstance. Secondly, we must believe and treat every worship service as a processional of victory and dominion, with the power to pierce the darkness and to discern the deceptions in souls of those assembled in the church (saved or unsaved) for every knee shall bow and every tongue shall confess one day that Jesus is Lord. Lastly, we must realize that worship is a covenant and that as we worship, with our all, heaven will back us with its all.

A few years ago, I was instructed by the Holy Spirit to create a network of true worshippers who would record and sing the Lord's songs. As you may have already guessed they are called Warriors in Worship. Yet, I strongly believe that God is raising up a last-day generation of worshippers within every nation, every state, every city, every church, every home, and in every willing heart, to become warriors in worship. I asked myself the following questions that you may be pondering yourself.

Do we actually engage the forces of darkness in these last days, personally? How do we participate in warfare? The answer to the first question is NO!! We, as mere humans, are no match for evil spirits, demons and the devil, but the weapons of our warfare are not carnal, they are mighty through God. They are not created by us alone. It is through the Spirit of God, working within us, that we do battle against the powers of darkness. It is very much like fleshing out Psalm 23.

A Psalm of David

"The Lord is my shepherd; I shall not want. He maketh me to lie down in green pastures: He leadeth me beside the still waters. He restoreth my soul: He leadeth me in the paths of righteousness for his name's sake. Yea, though I walk through the valley of the shadow of death, I will fear no evil: for thou art with me; thy rod and thy staff they comfort me. Thou preparest a table before me in the presence of mine enemies: thou anointest my head with oil; my cup runneth over. Surely goodness and mercy shall follow me all the days of my life: and I will dwell in the house of the Lord forever" (Psalm 23).

Notice in this text we are seated at a table. We are not warring, rather we are resting and fellowshipping. Jesus Christ is the Lord of Hosts of this spiritual feast, and we are being nourished and re-anointed for the battle we have come from, or will be going to. It is at the table where we see His glory.

It is at the table where we learn about worship as a covenant concept. It is like David is sharing the answer from the mouth of God to this question: Lord, will you be with me as spirits of death surround me? David says, yea and then he says, "I will fear no evil: for thou art with me." Church don't faint, He's with us.

Is the enemy attacking and surrounding you? Just activate your covenant by calling on His name. Your worship will change the environment, and it's going to explosively affect your situation for the better.

JUST WORSHIP KEY

In the midst of despair, just cast all of your cares on Him (Jesus) and worship Him.

Chapter Seven

WORSHIP IS A COVENANT

"When minstrels play and worshippers sing, the Prophet proclaims war in the heavenlies and the word of the Lord is exalted."

Allow me time to regress and share that true worship is found throughout the scriptures and can be located in practical poems, (or psalms) prayers, and prophetic voices. For more on this concept, look for my next book entitled <u>The Purpose of Poems, Prayers, and Prophetic Voices in Songs;</u> it will bless you too.

Worship is a covenant act in the spirit likened unto the physical act of sexual intimacy in the body. Oftentimes, many other cultures in Ancient and Common Era history utilized sexual intercourse as a religious act to appease the gods. This is why the bible admonishes us to avoid fornication because it's a form of idolatry.

We, being part of the Body of Christ, are connected to each other as Christians; therefore, if we fornicate, we sin against the whole body. We cause the entire Body of Christ to become in practice, though not in person, individually, an idol worshipper. Our altar of fragrance-scented praise and adoration is savored for another rather than to God Almighty.

Let's look at the results of covenant worship in the scripture. I really love this text that I am about to share with you because it is the very one God used to transform my life and to reveal His purpose of ministry for me.

"And the angel of the Lord appeared unto him (Gideon), and said unto him, the Lord is with thee, thou mighty man of valour. And Gideon said unto him, Oh my Lord, if the Lord be with us, why then is all this befallen us? And where be all His miracles which our Father told us of saying, Did not the Lord bring us up from Egypt? But now the Lord hath forsaken us, and delivered us into the hands of the Midianites. And the Lord looked upon him, and said, Go in this thy might,

and thou shalt save Israel from the hands of the Midianites: have not I sent thee and he said unto Him, Oh my Lord, wherewith shall I save Israel? Behold, my family is poor in Manasseh, and I am the least in my father's house. And the Lord said unto him, surely I will be with thee, and thou shalt smite the Midianites as one man" (Judges 6:12-16).

The chapter begins with the writer expounding on the fact that God's people had committed evil in His sight; therefore, God permitted their enemies to oppress them. When the angel of the Lord appears to Gideon, he addresses him as "thou mighty man of valour." I believe that although the nation was oppressed, God found that Gideon had not yielded his strength to the enemy by worshipping other gods. Still today, God's eyes are roaming throughout the earth, seeking for whom He can show Himself strong in.

"For the eyes of the Lord run to and fro throughout the whole earth, to shew himself strong in the behalf of them whose heart is perfect toward him" (II Chron. 16:9a).

Gideon continues on to doubt and question God's assessment of him, however, the bible tells us that, man looks on the outward appearance, but God sees our heart. (I Samuel 16:7).

Gideon was looking at his natural heritage as a limitation to his ability to accomplish the will of God, but God was preparing him to better understand his spiritual heritage and His omnipotent ability to perform wonders through Gideon's spirit man. He says to Gideon, "surely I will be with thee, and thou shalt smite the Midianites as one man." Certainly, Gideon could not defeat this numberless enemy by himself in the natural, but when we begin to receive and see an enthroned revelation of Jesus Christ, through worship, then we can obey the voice of the Lord and go in this knowledge: that all of heaven is with us, as it was with the generations before us.

In my own strength, I am a weakling, but in the spirit man, where God becomes one with me in covenant through worship, I am undefeatable. I abide in perfect peace and the creative power of the

Omnipotent one – Jesus Christ. He is the possessor of all power in heaven and in earth.

Further down, verse seventeen through verse twenty-four, Gideon is compelled to worship. He offers sacrifices to God to create a sweet smelling savour; this is typical of worship. Notice that as God responds favorably and comes to inhabit the offering (in the form of fire for our God is a consuming fire), Gideon is afraid because he encounters the very presence and peace of God. God makes a covenant relationship (Jehovah Shalom) with Gideon to officially document that this newly revealed altar would always produce peace, a covenant promise, rather than death as Gideon supposed.

What is the covenant relationship between peace and worship? First, as we accept the Lord, we have peace with God. Next, by the indwelling of His Spirit, we now possess the peace of God. Jesus says in John Chapter Fourteen, "my peace I give to you." Both refer to obtaining peace because we have accepted the new covenant of salvation through Jesus Christ, and we now are worshippers.

The next instruction from God to Gideon is extremely important. Gideon is commanded by God to destroy his father's pagan altar to Baal (a foreign god). Gideon was afraid to do this in the daylight, so he went by night. This is like most people today; they are ashamed and fearful to worship God before the world, so they do it in secret. But, if we are to displace principalities and powers, we must learn how to worship in spirit and in truth before the entire world – before doctors, judges, lawyers, mayors, presidents, saints, and sinners. The Midianites came close towards Gideon's village; however, verse thirty-four says that when this happened, Gideon by the Spirit of God blew the trumpet. What did he do? He worshipped! He gave the battle call for all Warriors in Worship to arise.

Now Gideon was prepared to train the rest of his men to do the same thing. First, he had to allow God to judge the hearts of true worshippers. Chapter Seven tells us that those who lapped at the water like a dog were only three hundred people, versus the other thirty one thousand and seven hundred, who were not approved by God. They (the three hundred) were given a pitcher with a light inside and a trumpet to battle the enemy. They symbolized filled human vessels with the direction, strength, power, and presence of God.

The trumpets typified worship or God's battle call instrument. How did they win the battle? Simply by worshipping! They were commanded to break their pitchers. The breaking of the pitchers spoke to the breaking of the outer-man, to let only the inner-man rule and reign. The battle cry was "the sword of the Lord, and of Gideon." Worship had released the offensive armor of God, which is the word of God. And Gideon's heart of a true worshipper had summoned the angelic company of Michael the Archangel, and his warring host.

My friends, this is how it is done – by just worshipping. Even in the midst of despair, simply cast all your cares on Him and worship. I know this from practical experience.

Before I go any further, allow me to share some personal and experiential thoughts about the power of worship in the wilderness and in the midst of your enemies. I want to use a sub-heading for this section entitled, "How to Get Out of the Wilderness."

I remember back in 1997, Theresa, and I along with our crusade team, were conducting a Shalom Crusade and Conference in Providence, Rhode Island, near the area of Boston. One night, there was a lady who came to the service who was from Boston. As I was closing the message of the preached word, I began to pray. I could discern in my spirit that this woman was oppressed by a demon in her soulish realm, the mind, will, intellect, and emotions - perhaps, nearing full possession. After praying, I started ministering to people prophetically. When I got to this woman, she started attempting to praise and thank the Lord, but the demon would not let her freely praise Him. The demon began using her mouth to sing a false and irky and screaming praise. As I began to minister to her, I first commanded the demon to be silent. Then, I prayed a prayer of deliverance over her. This agitated the demon and activated him to start muttering false praise once again. I instructed the musicians – keyboardist and drummer – to play in very high and loud notes and on the cymbals, as the anointing began to deal with the demon. The musicians were playing loud, cymbals were crashing, and the organ and keyboard was screeching a high note of praise. Soon after that the woman was set free and praising God in her own voice.

What I want you to see is that the notes and keys, as well as the song of high praise to the Lord vexed the demon. Worship brought vengeance upon the enemy and high praise silenced him. So how does this relate to worshipping in the wilderness and coming out of it? Well, Theresa and I had experienced a great financial challenge during this crusade, which put us further into a wilderness experience that we were already in. Yet, we still worshipped and fulfilled our mission to that state and the woman in the midst of our enemies. This is what the Psalmist saw and recorded in Psalm 149:1-9 and Psalm 150. I believe these two Psalms are unbroken and should be joined together to make one big declaration.

Psalm 149

"Praise ye the Lord. Sing unto the Lord a new song, and his praise in the congregation of saints. Let Israel rejoice in him that made him: let the children of Zion be joyful in their king. Let them praise his name in the dance: let them sing praises unto him with the timbrel and harp. For the Lord taketh pleasure in his people: he will beautify the meek with salvation. Let the saints be joyful in glory: let them sing aloud upon their beds. Let the high praises of God be in their mouth, and a two-edged sword in their hand; To execute vengeance upon the heathen, and punishments upon the people; To bind their kings with chains, and their nobles with fetters of iron; To execute upon them the judgment written: this honour have all his saints. Praise ye the Lord."

Psalm 150

"Praise ye the Lord. Praise God in his sanctuary: praise him in the firmament of his power. Praise him for his mighty acts: praise him according to his excellent greatness. Praise him with the sound of the trumpet: praise him with the psaltery and harp. Praise him with the timbrel and dance: praise him with stringed instruments and organs. Praise him upon the loud cymbals: praise him upon the high sounding

*cymbals. Let every thing that hath breath praise the
Lord. Praise ye the Lord."*

Notice in verse 9 of Psalm 149, it says "… this honour have all his
saints." What is that? The honour to be a warring worshipper.
However, just like healing, prosperity, and deliverance, not all saints
will participate in these benefits by their own choice. Again, it is by
praise and worship that all true believers can execute vengeance and
punishment upon the enemy. It is our chance to bind and chain the
powers of darkness.

One day while vacationing in North Carolina, the Spirit of God
spoke these words to me:

> When minstrels play
> And worshippers sing
> The prophet proclaims war
> In the heavenlies
> And the word of the Lord is exalted.

This was an answer to a prayer I prayed for clarity concerning the
ministry of music God had placed in my spirit and in my mouth.

This is the only chance in scripture that God allows us to get
revenge. You want to get the devil back for trying to mess with your
finances. Just start praising and worshipping God. You want to repay
him for trying to destroy your health, your marriage, and your family.
Just worship God. Go ahead sing a new song:

> **(Lead)**
> You alone be worshipped
> You alone be praised
> **(Chorus)**
> You alone do save
> Hallelujah, Hallelujah
> I will praise you all my days.

We indeed are Warriors in Worship. Child of God, stop taking the
devil's mess lying down. In a storm, worship; worship in the valley;

worship on the mountain. In the midst of despair, just cast all your cares on Him and worship Him.

Here are some of my final thoughts about true worshippers, music, and the role of warriors in worship in the last days.

What is the difference between a true worshipper and a Sunday-go-to-meeting worshipper? A true worshipper is blessed to have not only relationship, but friendship. Real worship is like having a best friend relationship. Take this scenario for example: My wife, Theresa; James, our mutual special friend; and my best friend, Preston Hughes and I enjoy and know each other's personality. We have a special way of interacting with one another. We would do anything in our power to make life richer, joyful, and pleasurable for each other. Let us say for the sake of this explanation (other than this being the case, it is almost impossible) that one or two of them (Theresa, James or Preston) are promoted to the job of the President and Vice President of the United States. Having the relationship and friendship that I do with all of them, I would be more apt to be invited to the White House than others (excluding the fact that I would be the first or second husband because of my wife), because of my past and current friendship and relationship with them.

Do you see it? This is how worship works. Not everyone is a true worshipper and not everyone is invited into the presence of God, based on their own friendship or relationship. However, if they are with a true worshipper, or with someone who has access, they can receive of the benefits and privileges of intimacy, friendship, and relationship.

Relationship and music are God's tools for creating intimacy in the earth. Music is intimately related to the nature of God. Music is the coded words of the heart of God. True Christ-centered lyrics are the decoded words of the mind and heart of God. I believe once these two elements come together in a marriage, you have recreated the real purpose of worship in music and Lucifer before he fell. (Isaiah 14:12). Music is furthermore meant to connect heaven and earth together. I believe that when Adam walked in Eden in the cool of the day, he heard music and lyrics. He heard the Lord's song. I believe Jesus Christ and the marriage of His bride will finally restore divine worship and praise. I believe when the anointing shows up in the church where true worshippers are - - a pre-wedding rehearsal is taking place. Jesus is the soloist! (Hebrews 2:1-2). And, if Jesus is the soloist, we will never have to worry about running out of wine, for He, Himself, is the originator of new wine.

Whether you are a pre-tribulation or post-tribulation believer, I believe that before Jesus returns on either instance, the Body of Christ will experience an awesome manifestation of prophetic worship, which will proceed miraculous and glorious outpourings of God's glory in unusual places. Everything has its own glory - man, angels and the heavens - but there is no glory like the glory of God on the word of God - Jesus Christ - to save wretched souls.

In the latter days, and these are those days, men, women, and children will love His presence and will continually dwell in the tabernacle of the Most High and all flesh will see His glory. And they will come to know Him, for only He, alone, is worthy to receive glory and honour, forever and forever.

Primarily, I believe I have laid a strong platform for worship, spiritual warfare, and music in this first book of the Just Worship Series. Now I want to talk mostly about the glory of God and conclude with some prophetic worship lyrics, which can be purchased separately on a compact disc (both instrumental and vocal). Already, you may have selected the book and music combination; whichever way you are receiving this word, I pray it will bless you, as well as prepare you for the days ahead.

JUST WORSHIP KEY

We crown Him Lord of Lords
We crown Him King of Kings
And He reigns alone
He sits high on the throne
And He alone is God.

Chapter Eight

IT'S GLORY: All Flesh Shall See It!

".. and all flesh shall see it together" (Isaiah 40:5a).

L ike many patterns and standards in the word there is always a prescribed order in receiving from the things of God. Just as there are principles which govern prayer, faith, and financial prosperity, so are there laws and patterns that govern glory. In this chapter, I want to share some prophetic insights into the God concept of His glory, and not only the "what of," but also the "why of" glory. Let's get started!

Primarily, we must recognize that God's glory ultimately is manifested in our midst because of His covenant and namesake. Glory is ever before us in His creation (heavens, angels, and mankind). However, not everyone recognizes, acknowledges, and comprehends it (Psalm 19:1, Psalm 8:5). But I believe, by the word of the Lord, that as the age of grace dwindles away, God will reveal Himself in such a way that all flesh will see and know of the glory of God. I did not say that all people would be saved. However, I did say that all flesh shall see His glory! Let's look at it from a different angle.

For instance, I can see Michael Jordan dunking a basketball on television, but I cannot do the same thing or become a professional basketball player, just by seeing him. In order to experience the joy and achievement of dunking a basketball, I would have to participate in the entire training and preparation of a professional basketball player. This is the same as it relates to the glory of God. In the last days, all flesh will see it, but not all flesh will necessarily participate and receive the spiritual, emotional, and physical benefits of the glory of the Lord.

Real glory is reserved for only those who want it. Glory is a covenant cut through the process of blood, fire, and water. The more our faith increases, the more our ability to see glory increases. When we realize that glory is the sole property and personification of God, and that it is forever in His power to withhold or to display, then and only then, will we be able to handle glory in greater degrees.

Let's take a look at a favorite passage of scripture. Almost everyone knows the disciple's prayer or what most people refer to as the Lord's Prayer.

"After this manner therefore pray ye: Our Father which art in heaven, Hallowed be thy name. Thy kingdom come. Thy will be done in earth, As it is in heaven. Give us this day our daily bread. And forgive us our debts, as we forgive our debtors. And lead us not into temptation, But deliver us from evil: For thine is the kingdom, and the power, and the glory, forever. Amen."

I want you to notice an established pattern and spiritual principle, as it relates to glory. In this prayer or text, the focus begins on God. He is exalted in heaven, and He is holy. As the text develops, the focus moves to our relationship with other human beings. Then, in closing the prayer, or in context, it reverts back to God as it ends by saying, "For thine is the kingdom, and the power, and the glory, forever. Amen." The point I want you to see is that God is the author and finisher of glory, and He owns it forever. As a matter of fact, He stated in the scripture that He would not share His glory with anyone.

"I am the Lord: that is my name; and my glory will I not give to another, neither my praise to graven images. Behold, the former things are come to pass, and new things do I declare: before they spring forth, I tell you of them" (Isaiah 42:8-9).

You see, we humans have the terrible habit of forgetting where we have come from and just as soon as God starts to bless us, we begin to praise and worship our blessings, instead of the blesser, Himself. God does not want us to give our praises to graven or handmade and man-made images or imaginations. Therefore, He speaks to us to remind us that the blessings and the things that we now possess were the former things that He promised to bring to pass, based on His immutable word. And, the new things that He is about to permit us to come into, He tells us or promises us, before it happens. If we would be totally honest with ourselves, we would realize that it was all God's grace and glory that brought us to the promised place. In our own strength and efforts, we failed miserably, yet God still used us and fulfilled His promises. Sometimes God forewarns us of some future danger, all to express grace and glory. In saying this, I want to give you a summarized statement of what I believe the scriptures reveal about the glory of God.

Glory is God going with us through the desert, the hard places, the crooked places, and still bringing us to the places of prosperity and fulfilled promises. The key elements which sustained us are goodness and mercy. When we look at all we have been through, start to finish – it's glory!

This God concept is repeated over and over again in the scriptures, especially in the ministry of Jesus:

- The story of the woman with the issue of blood for twelve years is a glory story.
- The men from the tombs of Gergesenes, who were possessed with demons (for only God knows how long), is another glory story.
- The man at the Pool of Bethesda, who was infirmed for thirty-eight years, is also a wonderful glory story.

If the scriptures were rewritten around our personal lives, many of our stories would also qualify as a glory story. Look at the following text briefly.

> *"And Jesus went about all Galilee, teaching in their synagogues, and preaching the gospel of the kingdom, and healing all manner of sickness and all manner of disease among the people. And his fame went throughout all Syria: and they brought unto him all sick people that were taken with divers diseases and torments, and those which were possessed with devils, and those which were lunatic, and those that had the palsy; and he healed them. And there followed him great multitudes of people from Galilee, and from Decapolis, and from Jerusalem, and from Judea, and from beyond Jordan." (Matthew 4:23-25)*

What I want you to see is that all of these people who came into contact, or had an encounter with Jesus in this text, were a participant in glory being revealed. And, when we look at many of the former encounters with Jesus, it did not matter how long it was from start to finish: twelve years, thirty-eight years, or like in the nation of Israel's case with Egyptian bondage of four hundred plus years, the grace and goodness of God is not confined, nor limited, by man's timeline. God holds time in His hands!

What is the decisive factor in the glory of God being revealed in all of these instances? Simply put, they all wanted to see and taste the glory of God for themselves. They all got tired of their own gory and sought after His glory. We will never taste glory until we get tired of self.

One of the most fascinating stories in all of scripture, to me, is the portion found in the Old Testament concerning Moses' request to see God's glory. Follow me as we examine some critical portions of this God-encounter.

> "*And the LORD said unto Moses, Depart, and go up hence, thou and the people which thou hast brought up out of the land of Egypt, unto the land which I sware unto Abraham, to Isaac, and to Jacob, saying, Unto thy seed will I give it: And I will send an angel before thee; and I will drive out the Canaanite, the Amorite, and the Hittite, and the Perizzite, the Hivite, and the Jebusite: Unto a land flowing with milk and honey: for I will not go up in the midst of thee; for thou art a stiff-necked people: lest I consume thee in the way. And when the people heard these evil tidings, they mourned: and no man did put on him his ornaments. For the Lord had said unto Moses, Say unto the children of Israel, Ye are a stiff-necked people: I will come up into the midst of thee in a moment, and consume thee: therefore now put off thy ornaments from thee, that I may know what to do unto thee. And the children of Israel stripped themselves of their ornaments by the mount Horeb. And Moses took the tabernacle, and pitched it without the camp, afar off*

from the camp, and called it the Tabernacle of the congregation. And it came to pass, that every one which sought the Lord went out unto the tabernacle of the congregation, which was without the camp. And it came to pass, when Moses went out unto the tabernacle, that all the people rose up, and stood every man at his tent door, and looked after Moses, until he was gone into the tabernacle. And it came to pass, as Moses entered into the tabernacle, the cloudy pillar descended, and stood at the door of the tabernacle, and the Lord talked with Moses. And all the people saw the cloudy pillar stand at the tabernacle door: and all the people rose up and worshipped, every man in his tent door. And the Lord spake unto Moses, face to face, as a man speaketh unto his friend. And he turned again into the camp: but his servant Joshua, the son of Nun, a young man, departed not out of the tabernacle. And Moses said unto the LORD, See, thou sayest unto me, Bring up this people: and thou hast not let me know whom thou wilt send with me. Yet thou hast said, I know thee by name, and thou hast also found grace in my sight. Now therefore, I pray thee, if I have found grace in thy sight, shew me now thy way, that I may know thee, that I may find grace in thy sight: and consider that this nation is thy people. And he said, My presence shall go with thee, and I will give thee rest. And he said unto him, If thy presence go not with me, carry us not up hence. For wherein shall it be known here that I and thy people have found grace in thy sight? Is it not in that thou goest with us? So shall we be separated, I and thy people, from all the people that are upon the face of the earth. And the LORD said unto Moses, I will do this thing also that thou hast spoken: for thou hast found grace in my sight, and I know thee by name [character]. And he said, I beseech thee, shew me thy glory. And he said, I will make all my goodness pass before thee, and I will proclaim the name [covenant] of the LORD before thee; and will be gracious to whom I will be gracious, and will shew mercy on whom I will shew mercy. And he said, Thou canst not see my face: for there shall no man see me, and live. And the LORD said, Behold, there is a place by me, and thou shalt stand upon a rock: And it shall come to pass, while my glory passeth by, that I will put thee in a clift of the rock, and will cover thee with my hand while I pass by: And I will take away mine hand, and thou shalt see my back parts: but my face shall not be seen" (Exodus 33:1-23).

The first thing that I want to highlight is that in the preceding chapter, God pronounces a judgment upon those who participated in the worshipping of the golden calf set up by Aaron after Moses took too long on the Mount of God. This speaks directly to the fact that God despises idolatry. He will judge it and judge it quickly.

Then Moses finds himself attempting to bargain with God over His righteous judgment to punish those who broke covenant and causes others to do the same. Sometimes, we should not do certain things in the sight of some people because they are depending upon us to show them the way. So God tells Moses, in so many words, that he has the ability to discern who deserves mercy or not. Why? Because he knows the heart of men, and he knows what we would do with the grace we receive. Some people are not grace users, rather, they are grace abusers. They have no real intention of following the will of God for their lives. They are idol worshippers. They worship themselves and their own ideas of life's philosophy. What's convenient for them is what they are going to do. God knew in this case with some of the children of Israel, so He told Moses that He must visit their or (this) sin. Idolatry is a serious sin because it seeks to give God's glory and worship to another. Nevertheless, since God is full of mercy, goodness and glory, He promised Moses that He would be there with them and with him, their ordained leader.

Moses was not quite convinced by God. Perhaps, because his natural mindset remembered how God dealt with the false gods and idols of Pharaoh. So he asked God for a sign of commitment as if His word was not good enough. We often talk about Gideon's fleece of wool, but we forget Moses' constant need for reassurance. God, knowing man's mortality, gives Moses the promise of His presence. If I can paraphrase it, I would say, Moses replies by saying, "if you don't do this, don't bother to send me because I am not going."

You see, Moses was familiar with meeting with God, as he did in his first encounter on Mount Sinai. It says that Moses hid his face because he was afraid to look at God. There, God promised to be with him (Exodus 3:11-12). Moses knew that without the presence of God, he was lost. He experienced the presence and glory of God before on Mount Sinai, and he knew that he needed it again in heading into the Promised Land. God reassured Moses again. This time, Moses says, to prove to me that You (God) would have mercy and grace on me, I need you to show me your glory again like you did before on Mount Sinai.

What exactly did this encounter mean? Well, I believe God's response is somewhat of a clue for us. First, God says, since I know you by name or since I am in covenant with you, and I know your character, I am going to do it for you.

What did God do for Moses after he requested to see His glory? He showed Moses His hinder parts or the latter portion of His Omnipotence in this situation. Let me further explain. It is like putting a DVD or video on fast-forward to locate the best part of a good heroic movie – the end. God placed him in a protected place of a rock, which is a type of Jesus Christ, and showed him all of His goodness and grace to deliver him through the entire length of his faith journey, from start to finish. Moses could not stand to see the full glory of God. It is just like when we get a revelation of God, and it is so awesome to our natural minds, all we can do is shake our heads, hold our heads, and shout, glory! True glory is too much for us to grasp. It's dynamic and explosive. If you have never experienced this, get closer to God and you will, sooner or later.

I believe Moses saw his good points, his bad points, his enemies and his friends, as well as his defeats and victories. God promised to proclaim the name of the Lord or His covenant sealed upon him by showing him grace and mercy. This is what God meant when He promised to cover Moses with His hand and show him His back parts. God's presence would be so close to Moses that He could literally touch Him anytime, yet He had to keep Moses in the rock of grace, or His glory would have consumed him. Real glory, like God, is a consuming fire. It would be that only after God had accomplished His will could He show Moses the final results of His workings. This concept, my friend, is what I believe is the glory of God being revealed to us finite beings.

Just in case you did not get that, Glory is God going with us through the desert, the hard places, the crooked places and still bringing us to the places of prosperity and fulfilled promises. The key elements which sustained us were goodness and mercy. When we look at all we have been through, start to finish and we see His message of goodness in spite of the mess – it's glory.

Remember earlier when I talked about man being crowned with glory? Just how is this accomplished? Well, primarily by accepting Jesus Christ as Lord and Savior. Jesus is the hope of glory. (Colossians 1:27). Without Jesus Christ there is no real glory in the life of man. Look with me for a moment at this scripture.

> *"What is man, that thou art mindful of him: And the son of man, that thou visitest him? For thou hast made him a little lower than the angels and hast crowned him with glory and honor" (Psalm 8:4-5).*

Notice if you will that a crown is usually placed on someone's head after they have triumphed in some type of conquest. So, the next question should be, what have we conquered? I would submit to you that we have conquered the process that separates those who are just seeing the results of glory from those of us who see and experience it, like Moses did. Seeing and experiencing are two totally different applications. The difference is found in the degree and level of outpouring. In addition, the process for being an experiential benefactor of glory is also different. Do you want to know the differences? I thought you would never ask. In order to elucidate this prophetic insight, we have to look at two passages of scripture of the same subject-matter recorded in both the Old Testament as prophecy and in the New Testament as fulfillment to prophecy.

Let us look at Joel Chapter Two, verses fifteen through eighteen.

> *"Blow the trumpet in Zion, sanctify a fast, call a solemn assembly: Gather the people, sanctify the congregation, assemble the elders, gather the children, and those that suck the breasts: let the bridegroom go*

forth of his chamber, and the bride out of her closet. Let the priests, the ministers of the Lord, weep between the porch and the altar, and let them say, Spare thy people, O Lord, and give not thine heritage to reproach, that the heathen should rule over them: wherefore should they say among the people, Where is their God? Then will the Lord be jealous for his land, and pity his people."

The point I want to make first of all is that we can see the results of things in the spiritual realm without really experiencing the process involved in getting to the result stage. Notice in the text that a significant move of God is preceded by a peculiar sound and a call for repentance and humility. Not everyone can see or hear spiritual things. Why is this so? Simply because their heart is not prepared to receive these things (II Corinthians 2:9-13). This is why Jesus always stated, "he that has an ear to hear, let him hear." And again, the scriptures say, "seeing we do not see and hearing we do not hear" (Matthew 13:13-17).

My friend, there is a primary difference in seeing and experiencing. It is the difference between the flesh and the Spirit. With my body I accept it; with my soul I believe it; and with my spirit I receive it. In order to experience something in the flesh, we must accept it in the flesh. In order to experience something in the spirit, we must receive it in the spirit. However, we can experience things in the flesh (physical realm), in the mind (soulish realm), and in the spiritual realm through the spirit because the spirit man is the ultimate base of control and functioning for our total being – spirit, soul, and body. Somewhat like a computer: the keyboard functions as the body. It is used to input or to transfer into the spirit and soul. Then, the monitor acts as a type of the mind; it's the place where we experience the mental image that we have accepted or will not accept. Finally, the hard drive is liken to the spirit-man. It is the base of operation, interfacing with the keyboard (body) and the monitor (soul). What we permit to go on in the spirit man will eventually make its way into the other two expressions of our lives.

Having said this, what type of experiences does it take to partake in glory? Well, allow me to restate an earlier statement that I made in order to tie things together. I said, real glory is reserved for only those who want it. Glory is a covenant cut through the process of blood, fire, and water. And the more our faith increases, the more our ability to see glory increases.

Look at verses twenty-eight through thirty-two in Joel Chapter Two.

> *"And it shall come to pass afterward, that I will pour out my Spirit upon all flesh; and your sons and your daughters shall prophesy, your old men shall dream dreams, your young men shall see visions: And also upon the servants and upon the handmaids in those days will I pour out my Spirit. And I will shew wonders in the heavens and in the earth, blood, and fire, and pillars of smoke. The sun shall be turned into darkness, and the moon into blood, before the great and the terrible day of the Lord come. And it shall come to pass, that whosoever shall call on the name of the Lord shall be delivered: for in Mount Zion and in Jerusalem shall be deliverance, as the Lord hath said, and in the remnant whom the Lord shall call."*

Notice that after the sound of heaven is heard in the beginning of the chapter, and repentance and humility takes place, then God promises to pour out His glory upon all flesh. The result is that we speak the things of God and we see the things of God. How do we get to these results? By going through the process. The process is explained in verses thirty and thirty-one. There are wonders in the heavens and in the earth; we experience blood, fire, and pillars of smoke. The blood speaks of the agent of life. We are saved by the blood of Jesus. What is the blood of Jesus? The life of God. It gives us a new nature or regeneration if you understand it that way. Whenever a believer goes through a trial or test we must be assured of the power in Jesus' blood. It is our only lifeline. The blood justifies us. However, it is the fire of God which purifies our inner-soul or character to become vessels of honor. God tries us in the fire in order to totally consume our lives. In order to be mightily used by God, His cleansing and purifying fire must consume our hearts. When we go through the fire, God proves our motives, faithfulness, and obedience. It is only that which is tried and true that remains. Then, with the refreshing water of His word, God puts out the fires in our hearts, minds, and soul - fires of confusion, misunderstanding and pride.

You know as well as I do what happens when water comes in contact with fire? It produces pillars of smoke. Notice that this theme is repeated over in the book of the Acts of the Apostles.

> *"And when the day of Pentecost was fully come, they were all with one accord in one place. And suddenly there came a sound from heaven as of a rushing mighty wind, and it filled all the house where they were sitting. And there appeared unto them cloven tongues like as of fire, and it sat upon each of them. And they were all filled with the Holy Ghost, and began to speak with other tongues, as the Spirit gave them utterance" (Acts 2, verses 1-4).*
>
> *"And I will shew wonders in heaven above, and signs in the earth beneath; blood, and fire, and vapour of smoke: The sun shall be turned into darkness, and the moon into blood, before that great and notable day of the Lord come: And it shall come to pass that whosoever shall call on the name of the Lord shall be saved" (Acts 2, verses 19–21).*

The blood, fire, and water process is repeated throughout scripture. This is a prophetic insight that I call the BFW process. It's also the route to glory. Moses journeyed through this process. When Moses is dealing with Pharaoh, a type of satan, he sees God turn water into blood, he sees a pillar of fire used to withstand the enemies' attack, and he sees water (the Red Sea) parted for him (acting as a refresher, protector, and restorer of dreams). (Exodus 7:20, 13:21-22; 14:16-26).

Let us look at another biblical illustration of this principle. We know the story of Shadrach, Meshach, and Abednego all too well, that we write it off as a fairy tale. I still believe that this, like all of the bible, is a true story.

We certainly can see some parallel truth in this story with regard to music in today's culture. If someone can get music to be the central and thematic focus of the trends of society, it can literally change and rule a culture. We saw this with rock and roll in the 60's. We are experiencing it in African American hip-hop music now.

> *"Then an herald cried aloud, To you it is commanded, O people, nations, and languages, That at what time ye hear the sound of the cornet, flute, harp, sackbut, psaltery, dulcimer, and all kinds of musick, ye fall down and worship the golden image that Nebuchadnezzar the king hath set up: And whoso falleth not down and worshippeth shall the same hour be cast into the midst of a burning fiery furnace. Therefore at that time, when all the people heard the sound of the cornet, flute, harp, sackbut, psaltery, and all kinds of musick, all the people, the nations, and the languages, fell down and worshipped the golden image that Nebuchadnezzar the king had set up"* (Daniel 3, verses 4-7).

Do you see satan? (Nebuchadnezzar is his type). He's trying to imitate God by making an attempt to be worshipped and to rule the hearts of men through music. We must recognize that in this life there is no neutral ground when it comes to worship. Either we choose to worship God by our actions, or we choose to worship the devil. This can be by fault or default, but just as the Rolling Stones once wrote in a song, "you got to serve somebody." We usually worship what we serve. I cannot speak for you, but I am not ashamed to let satan know that it is my fault or my choice to worship Jesus Christ. We should all be willing to follow the Hebrew Boys' example:

> *"Wherefore at that time certain Chaldeans came near, and accused the Jews. They spake and said to the king Nebuchadnezzar, O king, live forever. Thou, O king, hast made a decree, that every man that shall hear the sound of the cornet, flute, harp, sackbut, psaltery, and dulcimer, and all kinds of musick, shall fall down and worship the golden image: And whoso falleth not down and worshippeth, that he should be cast into the midst of a burning fiery furnace. There are certain*

Jews whom thou hast set over the affairs of the province of Babylon, Shadrach, Meshach, and Abednego; these men, O king, have not regarded thee: they serve not thy gods, nor worship the golden image which thou hast set up" (Daniel 3, verses 8-12).

This is usually how satan and his kingdom respond to those who will not participate in idol worship. My friend, a lot of times there are idol worshippers sitting next to you in the church pew. They won't lift their hands or their voices up to praise and worship the God whose breath they breathe. If you really want to show the world what kind of Christian you are, worship Jesus. For, if we lift Him up, He will draw all souls unto Himself. You don't have to be fearful of what the devil will try to do to you to force you to stop praising and worshipping God. Be bold and tell him, unconditionally, that you will not serve him. God has your back, your front, your sides, underneath you, and up over your head. This is what the Hebrew Boys knew to be true; therefore, they refused to bow down to satan, and God received the glory.

"Then Nebuchadnezzar the king was astonished, and rose up in haste, and spake, and said unto his counselors, Did not we cast three men bound into the midst of the fire? They answered and said unto the king, True, O king. He answered and said, Lo, I see four men loose, walking in the midst of the fire, and they have no hurt; and the form of the fourth is like the Son of God. Then Nebuchadnezzar came near to the mouth of the burning fiery furnace, and spake, and said, Shadrach, Meshach, and Abednego, ye servants of the Most High God, come forth, and come hither. Then Shadrach, Meshach, and Abednego, came forth of the midst of the fire. And the princes, governors, and captains, and the king's counselors, being gathered together, saw these men, upon whose bodies the fire had no power, nor was an hair of their head singed, neither were their coats changed, nor the smell of fire had passed on them" (Daniel 3, verses 24-27).

We must decide before the trials and tests of life come, who we are going to worship. This gives us the victory from the beginning. Even through the valley and shadows of death, we come out of seemingly hell, itself with victory and eternal life.

What I believe happened to the Hebrew Boys in the fiery furnace was death in virtual reality. They literally died to self-will, self-exaltation, and self-discovery. In a day where self-help and self-discovery is paraded around to be the keys of success and self-actualization in our society, God's word and ways tell us differently. In order to be used of God, we too, must die. If we die to self, then we can live and operate in His glory. God does not trust living people with His glory. He trusts resurrected people, meaning people who have died to their own agenda, but not living people.

Let us take a quick look at what I am talking about. I want to ask you a question or two. When do you believe Jesus decided to do the will of God? Do you think the Garden of Gethsemane was the place of final victory, or do you think it took place on Calvary? Jesus knew before He was born, before His ministry, before His mission, and before His mandate, that He would only serve and worship His father, God, and do His will. (Psalm 40:7-8). I believe this is the case also as it relates to the following text:

> "Then Nebuchadnezzar in his rage and fury commanded to bring Shadrach, Meshach, and Abednego. Then they brought these men before the king. Nebuchadnezzar spake and said unto them, Is it true, O Shadrach, Meshach, and Abednego, do not ye serve my gods, nor worship the golden image which I have set up? Now if ye be ready that at what time ye hear the sound of the cornet, flute, harp, sackbut, psaltery, and dulcimer, and all kinds of musick, ye fall down and worship the image which I have made; well: but if ye worship not, ye shall be cast the same hour into the midst of a burning fiery furnace; and who is that God that shall deliver you out of my hands? (Daniel 3, verses 13-15)

The Hebrew boys decided at this time that they were not going to v down.

Always remember that satan does not have the final say. There is a time period to your testing. The old saints used to say, "trouble don't last always." Yes, the devil will get mad and full of rage if you refuse to serve him. Yes, he will try to deceive you as well as seek to get you to compromise. He will seek permission from God to increase the intensity of your testing, but God will never permit you to be tested beyond that which you are able to bear. (I Corinthians 10:13). He will be with you in the fire. If you are going to ever become a true worshipper, you must learn how to bow down in the midst of the fire and let the fourth man – Christ Lord and master – get the worship. Then, He will also win the warfare for you and in you. Don't be afraid of the fire, it only comes to make you, and take you, higher in God.

I know what I am talking about because I have been in the flames of affliction for the sake of my faithful witness and for my worship to God. This is part of the process which requires personally knowing God and identifying with Jesus (Philippians 3:10). We must suffer persecution before we reign with Christ in this life as stewards and princes' of His glory. (Revelation 5:10). However, afterward, He revives us.

When God started refreshing and restoring me, after He took me through the blood and the fire, He first had to renew my mindset. I did not immediately recognize that I had been through glory because things were so bad for so long, that even after I endured all of my trials and testing, I was numb, battling bitterness and confusion. But I was ready for a new glory. Are you ready for new glory? We will see in the next chapter.

JUST WORSHIP KEY

Glory is God going with us through the desert, the hard places, the crooked places, and still bringing us into the place of prosperity and fulfilled promises. The key elements which sustained us were goodness and mercy. When we look at all we have been through, start to finish and we see His message of goodness in spite of the mess – it's glory!

Chapter Nine

A NEW GLORY IS COMING:
The Word of the Lord!

"Don't just be satisfied with seeing the glory, but be the glory"

God showed me the scripture of Jesus talking to His father and explained to me the following processes of Jesus' life and of David's anointing in order to renew and retain my focus on His glory. He was preparing me for a new glory. Glory is always coming, just like faith cometh, but it cannot be seen by all flesh unless we prepare it a temple to reside in. We are those temples, so let us get prepared. We must be Jesus minded and don't just be satisfied with seeing the glory, but focus on being the glory.

Look at this scripture with me:

> *"These words spake Jesus, and lifted up his eyes to heaven, and said, Father, the hour is come; glorify thy Son, that thy Son also may glorify thee: As thou hast given him power over all flesh, that he should give eternal life to as many as thou hast given him. And this is life eternal, that they might know thee the only true God, and Jesus Christ, whom thou hast sent" (John 17:1-3).*

What is this saying? God revealed to me that although He called me, and promised to use me mightily for His glory, that I still had to willingly be proven worthy of such a witness to His immutable word. His word is true, and it is forever established in heaven, but He wanted to prove to me that I really did believe His word. The hope of glory was in me when He spoke His promises to me. Jesus Christ—the Word—is the hope of glory. Hope is just a head dream until it is processed by our experience into faith and substance. In order for God to get anything kingdom: joy, healing, righteousness, peace, prosperity, and love - to you, He first must get it through you. It must be birthed in the spirit and fully received or engrafted into your spirit and soul.

God called and gave Jesus glory grace during His ministry – servanthood to His parents and to His fellowman. God gave Him glory grace during His missions unto the lost and hurting, and He gave Him glory grace during His mandate to taste death for all men and destroy the works of the devil (Hebrews 2:9; I John 3:8). Then He received that glorified state He once had with the father; that glory was already His from the beginning. He simply showed us the process of why it belonged to him. David's ministry was to feed the sheep, his mission was to slay Goliath, and his mandate was to establish the City of David (Jerusalem), and the Davidic order of the tabernacle. Only after he endured his trials and tests of cruelty, rejection, lack, and humiliation was he ready to handle the glory associated with his mandate.

I served many people, pastors, and bishops in ministry and as a missionary; I have traveled throughout the United States and abroad in Haiti. Yet, God sent me to Perth Amboy, New Jersey to Bishop Donald Hilliard, Jr. for him to speak into me and release me into my mandate – my command authority place in the kingdom of God.

Why there? Simply, he, as my spiritual father, has that authority himself because he has walked the length and width and depth of my mandate, already. He possesses the glory of my mandate to father me. It's not about popularity or status, it's about God's glory and us walking through the process. This is how it's done, by the blood, fire, and water process. But after the fire comes the water of refreshment: the ability to command in heaven and in earth, the power over death, hell, and the grave, and the floodwaters of depression, discouragement, and defeat. All of heaven and earth will come to know your name. You will have power in three worlds: earth, heaven, and hell. Just like the Hebrew Boys, after the fire comes promotion in the kingdom.

> "Shadrach, Meshach, and Abednego, answered and said to the king, O Nebuchadnezzar, we are not careful to answer thee in this matter. If it be so, our God whom we serve is able to deliver us from the burning fiery furnace, and he will deliver us out of thine hand, O king. But if not, be it known unto thee, O king, that we will not serve thy gods, nor worship the golden image which thou hast set up. Then was Nebuchadnezzar full of fury, and the form of his visage was changed against Shadrach, Meshach, and

82

Abednego: therefore he spake, and commanded that they should heat the furnace one seven times more than it was wont (normally) to be heated. And he commanded the most mighty men that were in his army to bind Shadrach, Meshach, and Abednego, and to cast them into the burning fiery furnace. Then these men were bound in their coats, their hosen, and their hats, and their other garments, and were cast into the midst of the burning fiery furnace. Therefore because the king's commandment was urgent, and the furnace exceeding hot, the flame of the fire slew those men that took up Shadrach, Meshach, and Abednego. And these three men, Shadrach, Meshach, and Abednego, fell down bound into the midst of the burning fiery furnace" (Daniel 3:16-23).

We must be like Christ: "I am He that liveth, and was dead: and behold, I am alive for evermore, Amen; and have the keys of hell and of death." (Revelation 1:18).

If we want the keys and power to unlock the effects of hell and death, we must die in the blood, fire, and water process and come back resurrected with the right attitude. For it is at the table, in the presence of God and your enemies, that we are fed the bread of the words of God, which we will later live by. We cannot be sent to a sin-sick world without seeing His glory, for we cannot reveal what we have not received ourselves. Just ask the Prophet Isaiah. Look at Isaiah Chapter Six, verses 1 – 8:

"In the year that king Uzziah died I saw also the Lord sitting upon a throne, high and lifted up, and his train filled the temple. Above it stood the seraphims: each one had six wings; with twain he covered his face, and with twain he covered his feet, and with twain he did fly. And one cried unto another, and said, Holy, Holy, Holy, is the LORD of hosts: the whole earth is full of his glory. And the posts of the door moved at the voice

of him that cried, and the house was filled with smoke. Then said I, Woe is me! For I am undone; because I am a man of unclean lips, and I dwell in the midst of a people of unclean lips: for mine eyes have seen the King, the Lord of hosts. Then flew one of the seraphims unto me, having a live coal in his hand, which he had taken with the tongs from off the altar: And he laid it upon my mouth, and said, Lo, this hath touched thy lips; and thine iniquity is taken away, and thy sin purged. Also I heard the voice of the Lord, saying, Whom shall I send, and who will go for us? Then said I, Here am I; send me."

We will have to go through genuine purification before we can really see our true self and realize that we are unclean and undone. We are a work in progress before a lost world; yet to God, the blood of His son, Jesus, presents us as holy and full of glory. After this we are sent to a lost people as witnesses. Christ in us is the hope of glory that fills the whole earth.

As I get nearer to closing this first book in this Just Worship Series, again hear the word of the Lord. He who has an ear to hear, listen and hear what the Lord says to His church by the mouth of His servant: (This word was originally spoken and recorded on a demo track in the early months of 1999.) "As we begin to enter into the next millennium, there is going to be an unleashing of a glorious anointing upon the church, which will be revealed in the people of God, that the world will not understand as it says in the text Isaiah Chapter Forty, verses 1-5:

"Comfort ye, comfort ye my people, saith your God. Speak ye comfortably to Jerusalem, and cry unto her, that her warfare is accomplished, that her iniquity is pardoned: for she hath received of the Lord's hand double for all her sins. The voice of him that crieth in the wilderness, Prepare ye the way of the Lord, make straight in the desert a highway for our God. Every valley shall be exalted, and every mountain and hill shall be made low: and the crooked shall be made

straight, and the rough places plain: And the glory of
the Lord shall be revealed, and all flesh shall see it
together: for the mouth of the Lord hath spoken it."

Isaiah begins to say it's time for the people of God to be comforted, for them to be encouraged. He begins to explain that there was a time of warfare. We are in war, but our warfare has been accomplished to the fact that we will now understand that we have the greater man inside of us. All of the saints of God will begin to understand that we are victors and not just victims. They will begin to understand the delicate balance of worship and warfare. We are Warriors in Worship. God will give us a greater understanding that it is His mercy and that He will have mercy on whom He will have mercy on. And that He will spread His loving-kindness throughout all the earth because it is Jesus who has saved us. It is Jesus who has strengthened us. And, He will begin to lift up all that which was low and in a valley. He will begin to bring down that which was high and exalted above the glory of the Lord, and the crooked He will begin to make straight. And, the glory of the Lord shall be revealed, and all flesh shall see it; for the mouth of the Lord has spoken it. By this I mean the King, the Sovereign King, the Lord, Jesus Christ; He decreed it, we begin to decree and declare it in the earth, and His angels begins to demonstrate it. Here is a prophetic prayer (I also received this word from the Lord in 1999 and I released it with a prophetic music single song entitled, "It's Glory"). All of the people of God will begin to understand that the glory of God is being revealed and just as in the Apostolic Church, the people are going to begin to look on us (those who don't know the Lord Jesus Christ) and they are going to begin to wonder why we have so much peace, why do we have so much joy, why do we have so much hope. And, we're going to say, such as I have, give I unto you. We will have in our possession the glory of the Lord.

"Father, we pray that you will begin to unleash a revelation knowledge, illumination of your glory. Let the church hunger and thirst for righteousness, that we may see and understand a revelation of your glory. The fact that You were with us in the beginning, in the hard places; that You went with us through the desert, and that Your glory is being revealed -- even now: that the Spirit of glory rest upon us and that You shall be glorified in the earth and all flesh shall see it."

The ultimate goal of every believer is to develop a lifestyle of worship. Praise is what we do to get God's attention. But worship is what we do and how we respond to a God who has come to give us victory, or as my father in faith and pastor, Bishop Donald Hilliard, Jr. says, "All of the answers to the most pressing questions of the new millennium are found in a simple: Yes, Lord."

So wherever you are today, whether it seems to be a good or a bad place, just worship and you shall experience His glory.

As I got closer to completing this book, almost two years later, the word of the Lord started coming to pass in New York City. The Spirit of God also reminds me of how He used me to foretell of buildings falling in the NYC financial district ten or more years ago. Yes, I am a native New Yorker, and I used to preach on the subway ride to and from my job in Harlem. Although this is in retrospect, God told me to write this to encourage the many other prophetic voices throughout the world to proclaim what you see and hear in the Spirit without shame. I can vividly remember the Wall Street employees who would tell me to be quiet and others would go into the next subway car only to see me a short while after I finished one message and went into another one in the next subway car. I pray that someone traded worlds.

JUST WORSHIP KEY

Glory is always coming, just like faith cometh. But it cannot be seen by all flesh unless we prepare it a temple to reside in. We are those temples, so let us get prepared.

Chapter Ten

TRADING WORLDS

"And he said unto them, ye are from beneath; I am from above: ye are of this world; I am not of this world" (John 8:23).

On the morning of September 11, 2001, the world as we once knew it changed forever. A group of fundamentalist Muslims, possibly linked to the alleged worldwide terrorist mastermind, Osama Bin Laden, terrorized the world by destroying the famous World Trade Center Twin Towers in New York City, and a portion of the United States of America military headquarters – The Pentagon. These heinous attacks that were almost perfect in their executions were no mere military offensive in so many respects, yet the attacks did speak a strong message to the entire world. I am deeply saddened by the countless number of lives that were killed on this dreadful day. The families, fathers, mothers, children, spouses, and friends of those directly involved will need a comforting voice for years to come. Let us be sensitive enough to be the hand and voice of God to these people. I admonish you to find some way to get involved and help ease the pain.

What these demented and demonized terrorists attempted to do was to let the world hear their voice which is a voice of evil, wickedness, and perverse imaginations. It was satanic! Hatred, fear, terror, envy, and strife are always seeds of satan. Therefore, we must look beyond the need for the fundamentalist Muslim, or any group of people, or a single person, to find their voice and see them as tools of evil. Everybody wants and needs a voice because this is what gives us meaning and significance in life. However, in this case we must look past the fact that their discontent with Israel and the United States of America is apparent. And, we must look further than the message they sent to the United States by attacking and crippling its financial, political, military, and social fabrics. The message said that although we (USA) are a superpower, we are not invincible. I believe God permitted this message to get through to the world and the United States of America. I also believe that satan utilized these yielded temples to deliver a message of not just hatred and evil, but as a signal of the intensification of his spiritual warfare against God and the kingdom of light. Do not be deceived for a moment; satan still wants to be worshipped. He desires to still have his name heard in worship and praise. So he devised a demonic strategy to sow worldwide seeds of fear. Why such a strategy? Well, satan knows the word of God too! "While the earth remaineth seedtime and harvest ..." (Gen. 8:22), satan knows that kingdom principles of sowing and reaping will work for the purpose of evil as well as for the purpose of good and God. Therefore, he has alerted his kingdom of darkness and demon spirits about the Mark 4:14 principle, "The sower soweth the word". The kingdom of darkness has sown evil in the likes of Osama bin Laden, Saddam Hussein and the Al-Qaeda terrorist network and now he is ready to harvest it in their wickedness. But, just like in the capture of Saddam Hussein, we win! However, the Body of Christ can do a lot to prevent some of their planned future attacks. We must first repent from our spirit of compromise and begin to speak the truth in love. We are gaining prosperity and things but we are deceptively losing our soul as a holy and righteous nation. We must return to the place to seek first the kingdom of God then things will be added to us by **Promise** and not by **Compromise**. We must strongly reconsider Mark 8:36 "For what shall it profit a man if he gains the whole world and lose his own soul?"

This strategy is not necessarily targeted against the world as much as it is targeted against the church. There is a spiritual battle that is increasing in the earth realm: a battle with spiritual seeds of faith versus spiritual seeds of fear. This is also a clarion call for the Body of Christ to increase its outreaches as never before. Let us pray for our President, political leaders, and the military, but we must not forget that God is providing us with the opportunity to show forth His grace and glory as never before. Yes, this was a terrible tragedy, and other worldwide terrorism events will continue to occur, but let us not forget that there was and will be a tremendous outpouring of God's grace and glory. Even in the face of moral, social and political decay, such as being displayed in the passing of same sex marriage act in America, God's word promises us this:

> *"Moreover the law entered, that the offence might abound. But where sin abounded, grace did much more abound" (Romans 5:20)*

On April 26, 2004, I received a visitation from the Lord in the form of a mini-vision which I later shared with my pastor and spiritual father. The Spirit of God prompted me to write it on paper that very day and I was obedient to the voice of God regarding this assignment. I have wrestled with the timing as to when this word should be released. As God would have it, knowing that in the mouth of two or three witnesses His word is established, when Pastor Rita Twiggs, a mighty woman of God from Bishop T. D. Jakes' church came to the Cathedral International, I believe I got a release in my spirit to share this word. Here is the mini-vision: There was a plastic bag filled with water and fish. Then I saw that there was a small hole in the plastic bag and the water was slowly seeping out. I began to cry as the Spirit of the Lord began to uncover and give me revelation about this vision. He said that the fish (souls of men, women and youth) would die, if the Body of Christ doesn't STOP and CONFRONT this strategic Spirit of Compromise that is invading our nation. He said that many churches will not be in this next move of the Kingdom of God. In 2005, it will be a year of Supernatural Grace and Truth, Apostolic and Prophetic Truth will increase within the Body of Christ. The Word of Truth will bring us and keep us in victory. ***Yes, we are called to be Victors rather than Victims.*** An increase of new Grace and Gifting will fall on us. The attraction of witches, adversarial spirits and divisions will increase but we will be victorious in all. It will be the best of times in kingdom advancement but the worst of times in persecution and a falling away. As I write revisions in this chapter in the ninth month of 2007, we are witnessing a continual unfolding of this word of the Lord. Yet, the Spirit of God declares "Look unto Jesus and not at men. The arms of flesh will fail. I will continue to filter and expose those who trust in their own righteousness. But, the truth will prevail."

We must not be caught up in the political and social ramifications of these historic acts of terrorism and same sex marriages and lose focus of the holy acts of God. Remember, in spite of what others believe, God promised to protect Israel and bless those who bless her and curse those who curse her. It is not merely about politics, but rather it is about a faithful covenant making God. God also promised to make the Arab nations a great people through Ishmael because of Abraham's ties with Hagar. Yet, Isaac who later fathered Jacob or Israel, is the son of covenant promise. My mother always said "God will never break a covenant. He will keep His word or we do not have to serve Him."

90

This is true, God cannot lie. Satan is the author or father of the lie but Jesus Christ is Truth and He sent the Spirit of Truth to protect the church during her finest hour. Remember, it is not just the USA's immigration policies which permit foreign non-Christian people to enter the United States, rather it's God's mercy and grace at work, so they can hear the gospel. But, we American Christians have become so comfortable with the world and the things of its culture rather than truly witnessing about Jesus the Savior of mankind. If we really want to find our voice as Christians we should return back to the times of street-witnessing and outdoor evangelism. It is in worship of the King of kings and Lord of lords where we truly gain the most powerful unilateral voice of purpose and promise of true life. We must remember that we are in the world, but not of this world.

This is what Jesus was saying to the Jews in the opening text of this chapter. "I am from above: ye are of this world: I am not of this world." We must not forget that God is not looking to start a worldwide movement of ecumenical cleric and people joining together for one purpose of peace and love. God is disgusted with relevant churches and Christians. When the true gospel is being preached, it's revolutionary and not relevant. The problem is that everyone wants to be like the other person and no one wants to be like Jesus. This is wrong! Jesus is our purpose. Jesus is our peace, and Jesus is our love. We only need to show the world Jesus, and He will save those who believe. Salvation is still of the Lord. We are admonished to be wise to win as many people of the world as possible, but we cannot compromise our message.

When I moved into a multi-ethnic diverse neighborhood in Piscataway, New Jersey, I was trying to move into another part of town, but it was not God's will. In my presumptions to please my wife, Theresa, and to offer my children the best house, I missed God. It cost my family and I a six month's stay in two different hotels and a lot of money. But God was faithful, and we finally moved into a single family house in Piscataway, not too far from a Muslim Temple and center. Every day, Muslim people lined the streets on feet and by car in route to the temple to pray.

God had put in my spirit to start interceding even before I ever noticed this Muslim Temple. Theresa and I would walk around the blocks interceding in our prayer language, then one day the Spirit of God spoke to me. He instructed me to go to the public library of our town and research the history of the town. To my surprise, the town use to consist of five of the neighboring towns that are now their own little towns. I found out that Piscataway literally meant the dark or dirt or the place of darkness. Then, God began to speak to me about this being a ruling spirit over this region. He also revealed to me the names of the spirits operating in these new or extension townships. Edison has a spirit of divination operating over it; South Plainfield has a spirit of death there; Dunellen has a strong spirit of heaviness or depression working over it, and Highland Park has a spirit of deception over it. All of these towns originated from Piscataway or the place of darkness. There are a lot of new middle and far eastern people moving into these areas.

In addition, there is a community of Jews who live in Highland Park. I believe God designed it like this. The point I want you to see is that God will upset and interrupt your self-willed plans to enlist you into the true work of a believer. He guided me here to be an intercessor for this region. God is about to show His grace and glory in Piscataway and all around the world. This is why I believe the World Trade Center bombing and terrorist attacks were permitted to take place. If God wanted to, He could have revealed their plans to the proper law enforcement agencies. I believe this act was permitted by God, and as a response to human evil, God literally guided sinners and Muslims to trade worlds during this time of uncertainty. Presently, many people are in bondage to a world of darkness but by seeing God's grace and glory throughout this tragic and many, past and future catastrophic events, they will be convicted by the Holy Spirit to trade worlds. Yes, we were startled by these sights of evil, uncertainty, chaos and fear but we as believers must fear no evil, for God is in the midst of us (Psalm 46:1-5). The world is looking at our response. They need to see our hope is in Jesus and not in the stock market, not in our jobs, not in our country, and not in our bank accounts. We should be able to point them to Jesus. Allow me to share with you some insights from the Book of Jude on surviving the last days.

> *"But ye, beloved, build up yourselves on your most holy faith, praying in the Holy Ghost, keep yourselves in the love of God, look for the mercy of our Lord Jesus Christ unto eternal life" (Jude 20-21).*

I want you to see a four-step plan of action that Jude gives us in order to survive the last and evil days. Yes, we will overcome terrorism, same sex marriages and any other evil plan the enemy designs.

First, we are encouraged to build ourselves up in the word of God or our holy faith. This in essence is the whole armor of God. We must be clothed and coated in the word to withstand these last days.

Second, we should learn how to pray in the Holy Spirit. We really don't know what to pray for, but the Holy Spirit does and will pray through us.

Third, we are challenged to keep our love hot. It is love that identifies us as Christians. Not our love, but the love of God which is shed abroad in our heart by the Holy Spirit. This type of love is toward everyone: family, friends, the faithful, and foes. Only God can give this to us for the asking.

Finally, Jude tells us to look for the mercy of Jesus Christ. Whenever you miss God, don't just go on and on without repenting and asking God for mercy. We as a nation need to look for the mercy of Jesus Christ unto eternal life. We need to repent of our increasing anti-Christ philosophies we have tolerated within the last two decades.

As I close this chapter, I want to share a song that God gave me in order to help me better process my emotions and feelings about the terrible tragedy we experienced on September 11, 2001.

Trading Worlds
(A response to the World Trade Center catastrophe)

One gloomy day in mid September
It was a day we'll remember
Would soon creep around the sunny skies
Demented hearts of evil lies
That hate could win and right human rage
Not knowing that it only heightens the stage

If men could see with the eyes of God
We would find love and not live apart
Torn and tattered
Scattered in heart
Lord forgive our sins
And by grace amend
Lord forgive our sins
And by grace amend

Tears flowing like an endless flood
The hurt, the pain and running blood
Feeling without hope, but not giving up
What display of love regardless of
If men would see with eyes of God
We would find love and not live apart
Torn and tattered
Scattered in heart
Lord forgive our sins
And by grace amend
Lord forgive our sins
And by grace amend

If men could see with eyes of God
We would find love and not live apart
Torn and tattered
Scattered in heart
Lord forgive our sins
And by grace amend
Lord forgive our sins
And by grace amend.

The song still brings divine perspective and healing to me as I sing it in my broken voice. How did you deal with this historic catastrophe? Can I suggest that you sing it too, read it aloud, or write your own song. Whatever you do, **Just Worship**!

This was just the beginning of my expressions of worship during this difficult period in our nation because soon, the leadership of our church would challenge us to reach out to the Arab and Muslim community in a Christ-like manner. The following is how God led me in this act of worship. I wrote down a prayer and evangelism note to distribute to Arab and Muslim-looking people. Here's a copy of that tract:

Hello, I am an American born Christian. In wake of the historic World Trade Center terrorist attack, you may be experiencing some acts of prejudice, hatred, fear, discrimination, unease, and rejection because of your race, religious beliefs, and your appearance of someone of Arab descent.

Therefore, I want you to know that I love you and so do many other true Christians, and I will be praying for the peace and safety of you and your family in America and in other parts of the World.

> *"God so loved the world that He gave His only begotten Son that whosoever believed in Him shall not perish, but they shall have eternal life" (John 3:16)*

My prayer for the Body of Christ is that these enormous evil and same sex marriages would be turned around for good by the display of Christian love everywhere. I hate to sound like a prophet of doom and gloom but evil and abounding sin will continue to visit our American shores with future catastrophic events, yet the Body of Christ will awake to her finest hours during these times. God will use us mightily to show forth His grace and goodness as never before. Being temples and channels of God's goodness, grace and glory is part of our purpose. As grace, favor and goodness increases on us, we must also increase in showing goodness to the lost and unsaved. Many people like to inquire of the Prophets of future events and what God is doing. The Holy Spirit has impressed upon my spirit this word of the close of 2007 and continuing into 2008, 2009 and 2010. ***The world will be going under and the church will be going up and growing up***. The Lord will be using those in the Body of Christ who understand this. Why? So, that it would be said of us as it was of the first century church, these men (women and children) have turned the world upside down. Glory to God! Then truly we will still be the home of the World Trade Center. Let us help others to trade worlds by showing them we still worship Him. In spite of terrorists, in spite of moral decay, in spite of unemployment, in spite of sickness, money in the bank or not and whatever we are confronted with, we can sing unto the Lord a new song. We can and we will Just Worship Him.

In order for the Body of Christ to become successful in helping others to trade worlds in the end times, we must regain this type of a divine concept of eternal purpose and glory.

The voice of His Majesty is speaking: Tsunamis, Hurricane Katrina and Rita, earthquakes in diverse places, as it is in the natural, so it is in the spirit. The bible says that these days would come (St. Mark 13:8). What else is the Spirit of God saying? God wants us to see that He is forever merciful. Although the earth is travailing and groaning, God is speaking expressly. He is speaking through nature, event after event and phenomenon after phenomenon. What in the world is God doing? I believe by the Spirit of the Lord that God is saying "All Eyes On Me!" Man has planned to rule and reign out of his corruption but the will of the Lord will prevail. His will is about to be done on earth as it is in Heaven. So what is going on in Heaven? Praise and Worship to His Majesty. Christ is seated in victory far above all principalities and powers, therefore, there is VICTORY in the Body of Christ! The Resurrection power emanating from His presence and the redemptive work of Christ is constantly being revealed in His body on the earth – the Kingdom people of God. We are supposed to be "The Hope of Glory Generation" showing and demonstrating to the world that Christ is in us (Colossians 1:27).

We are the generation where mercy and love are the methods of operation: God's mode of operation. If we don't understand this mighty revelation, we will be locked out of His end time covenant. The covenant and promise of glory is to explicitly show forth the praise of His Glory. God is showing that He is Alpha and Omega.

During this hour, everything that comes through our hand and possession is to help the world recognize that His nail scarred hands were stretched out in welcoming love and not wrath. The world must recognize that as He stretched His hands for us in submission to death, we must freely and willingly raise our hands in worship to Him. What do we do when the earth revolts because of sin? Just Worship! How does God expect us to react as the body of Christ when foreign godless nations attack our national interests? Just Worship! When we see the economy turn in a downward spiral, our response should be to come to God with an offering of worship. If we do, we will see the Kingdom of Glory manifested in everything.

JUST WORSHIP KEY

It is in worship of the King of kings and Lord of lords where we truly gain the most powerful unilateral voice of purpose and promise of true life.

Chapter Eleven

ETERNAL PURPOSE/ ETERNAL GLORY

"Yet if any man suffer as a Christian, let him not be ashamed; but let him glorify God on this behalf"
(I Peter 4:16).

Only eleven days after the World Trade Center attack I would experience the most painful and difficult time in my life. Even now as I place my pen on the paper, tears flow and my heart aches. You may wonder what can be so heartbreaking to invoke such a response? Did you lose someone in the attack on September the 11th? No, but many others did, and it pierced my heart and soul as well. However, I did lose a wonderful role model, a mentor, and a friend - my mother. Words cannot express how much I miss her. She was my inspiration for a lot of things. Mainly, the reason I am saved today and committed to the Lord the way I am is because of her example.

If I ever needed to understand or grasp eternal purpose, I only had to think about my mother's life and her lifestyle. How could I have known that the Lord would take her before I finished this book? Yet, it was her sudden departure from a life of suffering and victory that has motivated this chapter. I say that she is still teaching me in her death. During her home going service we shared with hundreds, and now you, the reader, **the reflections of her lifetime:**

"As God was walking through the garden of this world admiring His beautiful flowers, He stopped to choose a special orchid, one that had withstood the winds of time. On Saturday, September 22, 2001, Prophetess Maggie Bell Williams Deaver was plucked from the garden and took her place in eternal glory.

Maggie Bell Williams Deaver was born April 23, 1928, to the late Rev. Norman Williams Sr., and Rossie Lee Williams. She was educated in the Pender County, Rocky Point, North Carolina school system. Maggie Bell grew up under strong Christian principles. She was united in marriage to Roland James Deaver. They were blessed with eight children.

Maggie Bell relocated to Brooklyn, New York during the 1950's Afro-American Northern emigration. She joined the United Pentecostal House of Prayer under the Pastorate of the late Bishop Lucille Allen. She received Jesus Christ as her personal Savior and continued to grow in grace. Maggie Bell remained a faithful active member for over 40 years.

Heeding a higher calling, she accepted the next level of ministry and was ordained an Elder. She attended Bethel Bible Institute and received ministry credentials in Evangelism. After the untimely death of Bishop Lucille Allen, Elder Maggie Bell Deaver joined St. Paul United Church of God, Brooklyn, New York under the leadership of her sister, the late Pastor E. M. Shiver.

She walked in the office of a prophet and was used mightily by God to: foretell, forth-tell, share words of wisdom and knowledge, call forth life into dead situations and speak inspired prophetic utterances into the lives of countless individuals.

Elder Deaver was a *no-nonsense* person, a preacher of the Gospel, a praying woman, devoted mother and grandmother, loving sister, a caring aunt and friend to the masses. When she gave you a prophetic word you could **Take It To The Bank**! Her favorite saying was '*If God said it - I will stake my life on it.*'

Her sudden catching away leaves a great void in the lives of her children, grand-children, the Williams/Deaver family, Church family and all who had the occasion to know her.

Elder Maggie Bell Deaver was preceded in death by her husband, Roland James Deaver and her son James Roland."

My mother, as you have learned and will read more of, was an extraordinary person. She epitomized to many the scripture in Ephesians chapter one and verse twelve:

> *"That we should be to the praise of his glory, who first trusted in Christ."*

It was with this conviction that she was reared, and it is the same conviction from which she raised me and seven siblings. We were taught that we were made to worship the Lord in spirit and in truth. However, even though you are nurtured one way, salvation is something you don't comprehend until you receive it for yourself. It's not a religion; rather it is a genuine relationship. My mother's favorite song was "I Know Jesus." She reared us to fulfill this as our highest goal in life. Please permit me to highlight and color in some of the empty spots in my mother's life that will give greater context to this chapter and permit you to see why she had to be in this book.

First, my mother was a second generation preacher. Out of a large number of thirteen siblings, only four of them were not directly involved in the ministry in one way or another. Secondly, my father preceded my mother in death due to his alcoholism and physically abusive behavior towards my mother. In defense of his mother, my oldest brother accidentally mortally wounded my father - a father who I never saw, because Momma was two months pregnant with me. She went on to raise eight children as a single parent. I am the youngest of the eight and the first to receive salvation. Yes, I am a Momma's boy. Gloriously, I was also used by God to help pray with my oldest brother who is now saved and working in the kingdom of God as a deacon. Today, most of my siblings are saved. Glory to His mighty name!

I can remember how Momma would bring all of us – five boys and three girls around her bed for prayer every Sunday morning before she took us to Sunday School. We did not have a car; we would have to take the train, bus or a taxi cab. It would get me angry when I could not ride in the taxi cab because Momma had gathered a group of neighborhood children to take to Sunday School with us. Whatever way we got there, we had to be there. This was her pattern, her standard, and her purpose. She was determined to show us the gospel rather than just preach to us and teach us. Later on, as we all matured and left home, whenever we talked to her she would always want to know if we were attending church. I recall when I accepted the Lord at South Carolina State University, I would call her and tell her to pray for me constantly until one day she surprisingly told me to pray for myself. She replied, "You pray, you know how to pray." Yes I did know how to pray because she had taught me. She showed us all how to pray, how to cook, how to clean house, how to wash, iron and fold clothes, and how to sacrifice for your children. Not only did she do this for her children, but also for her thirty-two grandchildren and her sixteen great grandchildren.

She had a true sense of eternal purpose and would lay down her life for her seed. I can humbly state I am the only child to graduate from a university. Although my mother was employed as a domestic worker for Jewish families, she used faith and those funds to raise eight children and to put me through college. In addition, she encouraged my brothers and sisters to be a financial support for my college education. For this I am very grateful and thankful for my family.

Momma never remarried, although she often said that she would. Instead, she was the solid rock for many Christian leaders who came to her for prayer and a word from the Lord. Momma, as we all called her, never even accepted an invitation from a man to go out on a date. She did not have any undercover romances, nor did we have any fake uncle Charles paying our bills and sleeping over at our house. She raised us to be full of faith and to be full of the fear of God. She was a virtuous woman for sure. Her favorite saying to me was, "Whatever you do in the Lord's house, let it be real." I will always cherish those words and seek to obey them too.

This is primarily why I am a worshipper today because my mother was my first teacher. Before I ever learned or was exposed to a new paradigm of worship, I was privy to a lifestyle of worship at home as a child. As the content suggests, Maggie Bell Deaver suffered as a once battered wife and later a single parent, raising eight children on public assistance, yet she was not ashamed to let people know that she was a tither. In spite of the fact that we struggled financially, this did not hamper my mother's love because she would feed the neighborhood children and take some of them to church along with us. She was a true evangelist. Whenever she did not see a way, she would pray a way up, and God would faithfully meet our needs. Momma understood eternal purpose, indeed.

Being that I am university trained, I was able to subjectively devise my own concepts of purpose. I believe that purpose and destiny are progressive in nature. First, it is confined or hidden within us. Secondly, purpose is defined or revealed to us gradually, and finally, it is refined or polished and made perfectly clear. Yet, with all of my training and education, I have not embraced my eternal purpose with the same fervor and vigor that I have witnessed in my mother. She never complained about her Christian responsibility or blamed God. Through the good and the bad, when times were wonderful, and when times were dreadful, she would simply Just Worship. I can hear her now singing "I Know Jesus." Almost nothing could keep her from worship services and three generations later, she was still teaching the next generation how to pray before going to Sunday School. It is without question that you know that I loved her dearly and that I am going to miss her greatly, nevertheless, I am rejoicing in the fact that she is in eternal glory.

God spoke to me during this critical time in my life, and He said that my mother lived a life of glory. Her life was a word picture of glory. Not only did she teach me about cooking, sewing, shopping, paying bills, loving your enemy, being truthful and honest, she taught me about glory. Yes, Momma taught me how to Just Worship and that Jesus is the glory and lifter up of my head. She taught me about eternal purpose and eternal glory. In closing this chapter, I want to give some scripture verses that I believe best characterized her life and her death.

As a true prophetess, this was her mindset:

> *"If ye be reproached for the name of Christ, happy are ye; for the Spirit of glory and of God resteth upon you: on their part he is evil spoken of, but on your part he is glorified" (I Peter 4:14).*

As an elder stateswoman, in the Body of Christ, and as a mother in Zion, she exemplified this text:

> *"The elders which are among you I exhort, who am also an elder, and a witness of the sufferings of Christ, and also a partaker of the glory that shall be revealed" (I Peter 5:1).*

As a person who understands eternal purpose and eternal glory:

> *"For our light affliction, which is but for a moment, worketh for us a far more exceeding and eternal weight of glory" (II Corinthians 4:17).*

And finally, as a faithful servant who finished her course and has gone from labor to her eternal reward:

"But we all, with open face beholding as in a glass the glory of the Lord, are changed into the same image from glory to glory, even as by the Spirit of the Lord" *(II Corinthians 3:18).*

Although my mother is no longer here on earth with us, I know for a fact that she is with the Lord. I will miss her and I will weep over her absent personality in flesh, yet I will worship the Lord because she is resting in the eternal glory. Hallelujah!

JUST WORSHIP KEY

I was taught that we were made to worship the Lord in spirit and in truth. However, you may be nurtured one way but salvation is something you don't comprehend until you receive it for yourself.

Chapter Twelve

PROPHETIC WORSHIP

In this last chapter, I want to share some prophetic worship songs that I have stewarded from the throne of God. Many of these songs are published in music form to accompany this book or they will be, or have been, published on other projects. This is just the first volume of the Just Worship series, and I have a soon to be released book entitled The Purpose of Poems, Prayers, and Prophetic Voices, which will also have a CD project with songs sung by various artists from the Warriors in Worship Prophetic Company.

Most of these songs were birthed in a season of intensive spiritual warfare. The battles had become heated and the test and trials not a few. Yet, remaining faithful and committed to the crosswalk, I was rejoicing in the midst of the conflict. I was at home, and unemployed at this time. It had been revealed to me by the Spirit of the Lord that I had achieved a manifested position of dominion and authority in the spirit realm regarding the enemies' attack on my family, my finances, my faith, and my city. As previously stated, I have since learned that God had sent me to this town on assignment as an intercessor.

The following lyrics are what the Spirit of God began to say through me, and to me, and the songs that I released into the heavenlies.

PROPHETIC WORSHIP

Warriors in Worship

By Steven E. Deaver

Arise, all ye warriors
(Repeat)
All ye warriors, arise
(Repeat)

[Unison]

with the sword of the Lord
we will sound our battle call
as we enter the heavenly doors
let the chains of bondage fall to the floor
oh, let the chains of bondage fall

Arise, all ye warriors
(Repeat)
All ye warriors, arise
(Repeat)

for where the Spirit of the Lord is there is liberty
for where the Spirit of the Lord is the captives are set free
as we enter the heavenly doors
let the chains of bondage fall to the floor
oh, let the chains of bondage fall

let the chains of bondage fall to the floor
oh, let the chains of bondage fall
oh, let the chains of bondage fall
oh, let the chains of bondage fall

[Leader]
SHOUT unto the Lord with a voice of triumph for our God has given
us the city.

Your Honor
By Steven E. Deaver

Your Honor
I come before Your throne
There is something really wrong
I must confess to You
But before I present my case
I don't come with merits
It's all about Your grace
Nothing that I have done
Nothing that I have done
So before I even start
I know You know my heart
I bow down, and say
Have mercy on me this day

I plead the blood of Jesus in this case
I plead the blood of Jesus in this case
I plead the blood of Jesus in this case
I need Your mercy and I need Your grace
I plead the blood

I know I have fallen short
Forgive me of my transgressions
By the blood and I make my confession
I plead the blood of Jesus in this case
I plead the blood of Jesus in this case
I plead the blood of Jesus in this case
I need Your mercy and I need Your grace
I plead the blood
Your Honor, the blood is my defense

PROPHETIC WORSHIP

Breathe On Me

By Steven E. Deaver

Lord, I am empty
And I need to feel Your Spirit
Things seem dry, callous, and cold

Lord, I'm hungry and thirsty for Your presence
I need joy and restoration of my soul

Breathe on me
Breathe on me
Holy breath of God

Breathe on me
Breathe on me
And let Your Spirit fill my heart

THE JUST WORSHIP SERIES

Just Worship

By Steven E. Deaver

I know things are not going right
satan's putting up a fight
With tears in your eyes, no money in the bank
You feel like giving up

Don't let it get you down
Pick your head up from the ground
And give God praise, now and always
Give Him praise

(2x)

Just worship, Just worship
Just worship, Just worship
In the midst of despair
Cast all of your cares, and worship, worship Him

Pain in your mind
And your bills are due
No one is willing to help, help you through

Though your back's against the wall
He won't let you fall
The Lord Jesus is going to see you through
He knows what to do

Just worship, Just worship
Just worship, Just worship
In the midst of despair
Cast all of your cares, and worship, worship Him
Cast all of your cares, and worship, worship Him

Just Worship (continued)

(Vamp)

109

PROPHETIC WORSHIP

Your praises will silence the enemy
your worship will set the captive free

In the midst of despair
Cast all of your cares, and worship, worship Him
And worship, worship Him

Just worship, Just worship
Just worship, Just worship

THE JUST WORSHIP SERIES

I Love Your Presence

By Steven E. Deaver

Oh, how I love Your presence
Oh, how I love Your presence
Oh, how I love Your presence
It's You Lord who I desire

Oh, how I love Your presence
Oh, how I love Your presence
Oh, how I love Your presence
It's You Lord who I desire

You are sweeter than honey
You are better than silver
More precious than gold
It's You Lord who I desire
It's You Lord who I desire

You are sweeter than honey (sweeter than honey)
You are better than silver (better than silver)
More precious than gold (precious than gold)
It's You Lord who I desire
It's You Lord who I desire

(Bridge – 3x)

I searched high and low
It is you oh, I know
It is You Lord who I desire

Oh, how I love Your presence
It's You Lord who I desire
It's You Lord who I desire
It's You Lord who I desire

111

PROPHETIC WORSHIP

Teach Me How To Worship

By Steven E. Deaver

Teach me how to worship
And truly honor Thee
And not what I think
What worship should be
Help me get past the outer courts
Come behind the veil
From deep down within my spirit
Let there be a holy travail
Let me judge myself by the mirror of Your word
Let me seek Your mercy and grace
Teach me how to worship You, Lord face to face
Teach me how to worship you, face to face

(Bridge)
I want to worship you, face to face
I want to worship You, and receive more of Your grace
Let the words of my mouth
And the meditation of my heart
Be acceptable, oh Lord, teach me how to worship

(Vamp)
I want to worship (Worship)
I want to love you (Love you)
In the beauty of holiness (Holy)
With my hands lifted high and my heart in the right place
Let me receive more of Your grace

I want to worship you, face to face
I want to worship You, and receive more of Your grace
Let the words of my mouth
And the meditation of my heart
Be acceptable, oh Lord, teach me how to worship

112

Teach Me How To Worship (continued)

Let the words of my mouth
And the meditation of my heart
Be acceptable, oh Lord, teach me how to worship

That's How Love's Supposed To Be

By Steven E. Deaver

He gave His life
He sacrificed
He showed us how
To live our lives
Without complaint
Or any doubt
That's how love's supposed to be
That's how love's supposed to be

He carried His cross
He paid the cost
And oh what a price
A selfless life

(Chorus)

We're covenant partners
We're lovers for life
Serving each other
Selfless sacrifice

Without complaint
Or any doubt
He showed us how
We should live our lives
That's how love's supposed to be
That's how love's supposed to be

Me serving you and you serving me
That's how love's supposed to be
That's how love's supposed to be

114

JUST WORSHIP KEY

Worship is the reason we exist!

Postlude

By Steven E. Deaver

O Lord Most High
O Lord Most High
Rock of Ages, El Shaddai
We praise You O Most High.

O Lord Most High
O Lord Most High
Rock of Ages, El Shaddai
We praise You O Most High.

We praise You O Most High
We praise You O Most High

You're the Almighty Holy One
El Shaddai we praise You O Most High.

Doxology

By Steven E. Deaver

It's glory, it's glory, it's glory, it's your glory
It's glory, it's glory, it's glory, it's your glory
The angels bow down and worship Thee
Because you're pure, Holy and full of majesty

Your glory, Your glory, Your glory in creation
For you alone are worthy, Lord, for this
great demonstration
For you alone are worthy, Lord, to be praised
of every nation
For you alone are worthy to receive exaltation
You alone are worthy, Lord, for this
glorious manifestation.

BENEDICTION

Until next time, remember that through the good and the bad, and in the midst of despair, cast all your care on Him and Just Worship Him.

"Now unto Him that is able to keep you from falling, and to present you faultless before the presence of His glory with exceeding joy, to the only wise God our Savior, be glory and majesty, dominion and power, both now and forever. Amen" (Jude 24, 25)